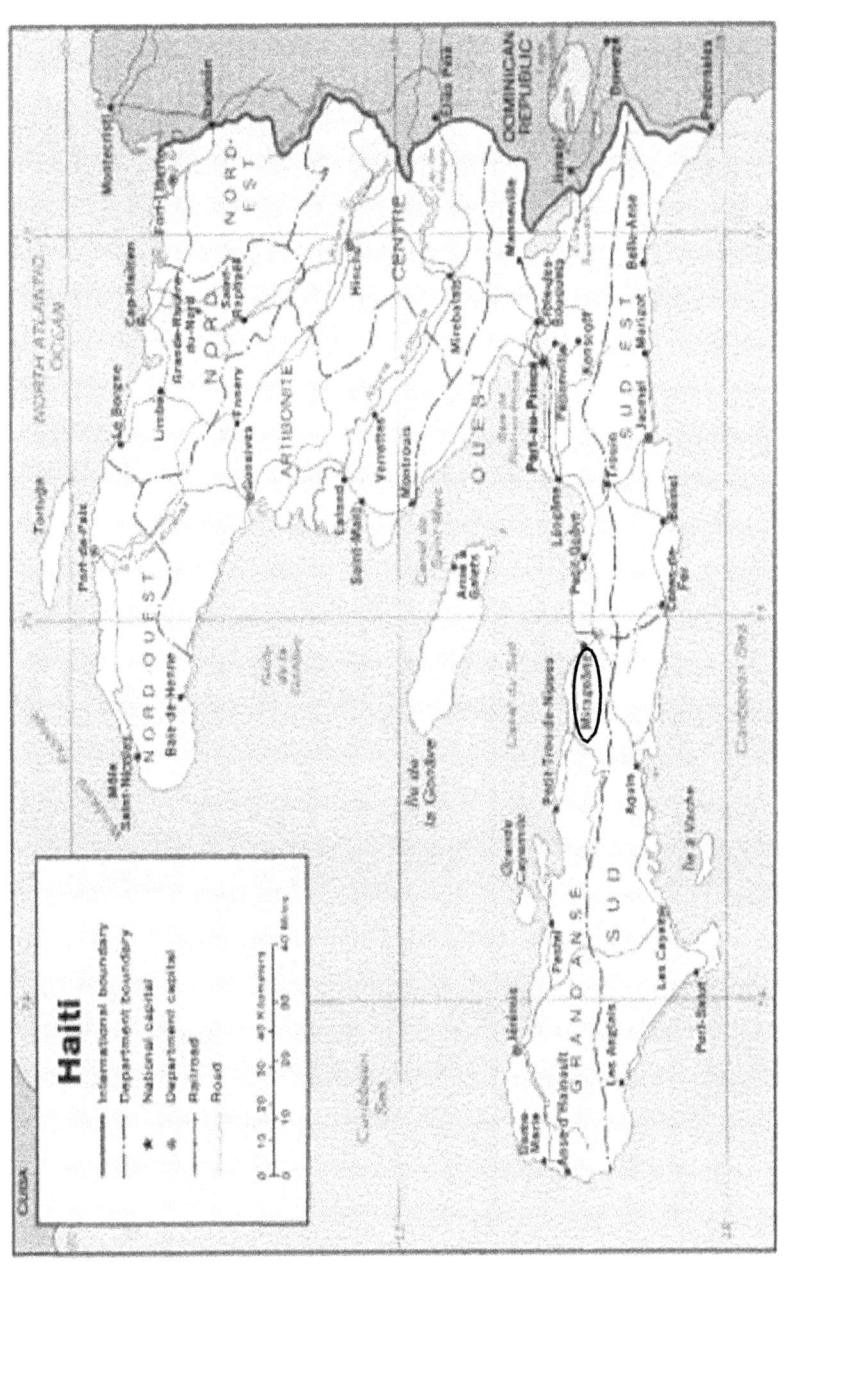

Tale of a multifaceted life
by Enice Toussaint

Volume 1

Éditions Nouveau Siècle

ISBN: 978-2-9823179-3-2 -ebook

Handing in – 1er trimester 2025

Copyright

Bibliothèque Nationale du Québec

National Library of Canada -ebook

In memory of my mother.

For my children Natatsha and Max who helped me realize this writing project.

To my grandchildren whom I adore.

May they cherish the memory of each life

and thus learn perseverance.

Your life can be filled with joys and satisfactions. We cannot allow obstacles to destroy well-being and happiness. We are defeated only if we accept defeat.

Martin Gray
The Book of Life

Table of Contents

Foreword 3
Foreword 4
Prologue 6
    May 16, 1989 6
    Saturday, April 27, 1997 7
    May 3, 1997 8
    May 21, 2000 8
1 10
First Life 10
A Happy Childhood 10
    Irène, Robert, and Me 14
    Our Childhood Games and Bond 16
    Sweet Memories 16
    Reflection 17
    In School 18
    The Journey to and from School 19
    School Life and Memories 19
    Reflections 20
    Nounoune and Holidays 21
    New Year's Day Celebrations 22

    A Less Joyous Holiday: Mardi Gras 23

    Reflections 23

    Mother's Death 24

    Her Final Hours 25

    The News 25

    Unspoken Fears 26

    Legacy of Loss 27

2 29

Second life 29

After Mama's Death 29

    Life After Mama's Death 31

    A New Chapter 32

3 34

Third Life 34

Aunt Anna's House 34

    A Difficult Year 35

    A Betrayal Uncovered 36

    The Journey Home 36

    Confrontation and Resolution 37

    Reflections 38

4 39

Fourth life 39

Return to Miragoâne 39
    At Aunt Dieula's Home 40
    First Love 40
    A Dream That Changed Everything 41
    A New Beginning 42
5. 44
Fifth life 44
With the Nuns 44
    My Arrival at the Convent 45
    Rediscovering Joy 45
    A Beacon of Light 46
    A Safe Haven 47
    The City of Miragoâne 47
    My Life with the Sisters 49
    An Unexpected Encounter 56
6. 60
Sixth life 60
A Sad Marriage 60
    Newlywed in Miragoâne 61
7. 68
Seventh life 68
A Secret Love 68

  The Beginning of a Double Life 71

8 82
Eighth life 82
Hardships in The United States 82
  First Steps in New York 83
  Hardships in New York 88
  A Secret Meeting 92
  Nanny in Connecticut 96

9 100
Ninth Life 100
Passage Through Haiti 100

10 109
Tenth Life 109
From Haiti To Montreal 109
  Longueuil 123
  Jacques in Montreal 126

11 130
Eleventh Life Between Two Men 130
  Happiness, Sadness, and Love 131
  The Fruit of Love 135
  Another Move 140
  A Difficult Pregnancy 143

  The Birth of My Daughter 146
  Natatsha's Baptism 151
  Back to My Business 156

12 161

Twelfth Life 161

Towards Liberation 161

  In Ville d'Anjou 162
  Some New Changes 166
  The Separation 169

 Epilogue 174
 A Conclusion of Sorts 174
  Generic 177
  Generic 180
  Generic 184
 Acknowledgements 188
 Readers' Comments 190

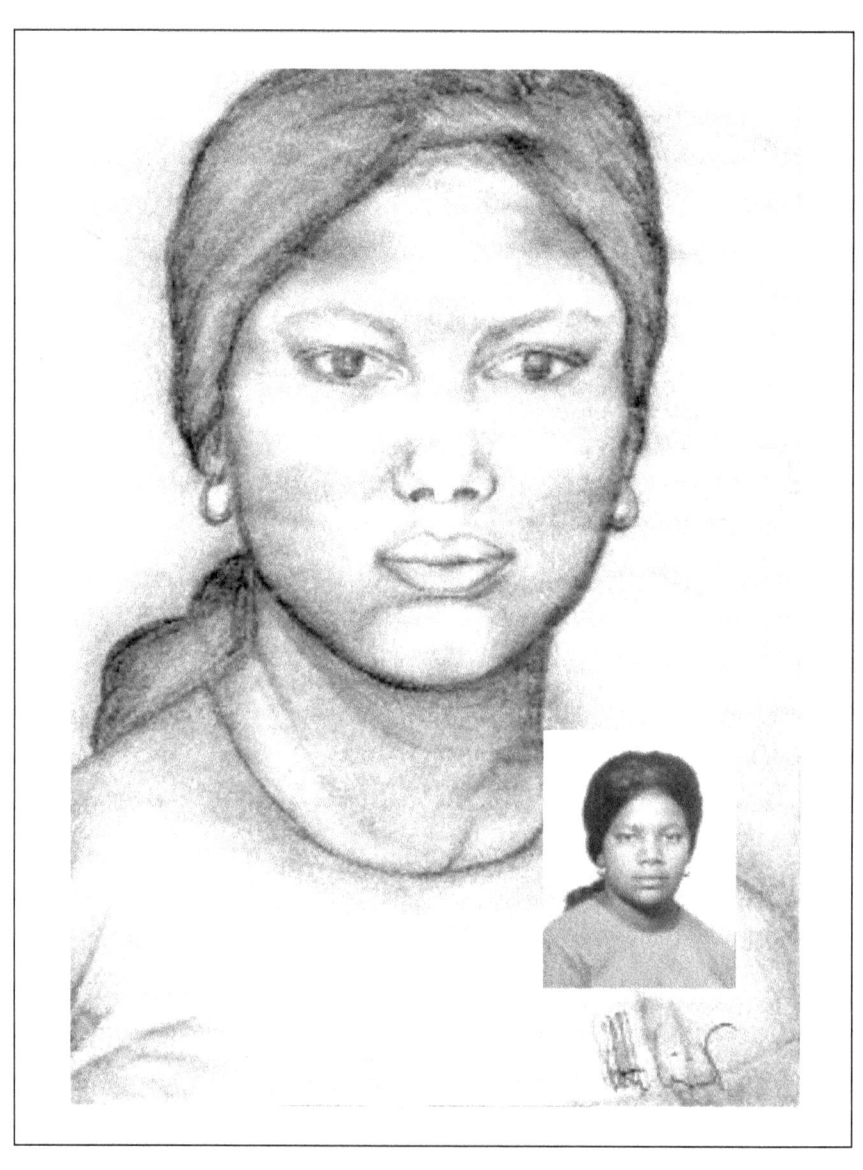

Drawing of Enice by her daughter Natatsha, 1997

This book is based on a true story.

All names of the characters mentioned are fictitious.

Foreword

As your heart goes out to this —Woman Amongst Others, ‖ her endearingly inspiring and honest sharing bridges the path to a compassionate humanity. With each unadorned revelation of her struggles and choices, her unwavering faith, growing strength, and determination mirror back your very own dormant potential. So that when the last word is spoken, the last page is turned you realize that all along, something miraculous has been happening. You have done more than just read a book. You have also journeyed within yourself and, by the grace of God and this courageous woman, come full circle home to the recognition of the person you were truly born to be.

That is the power and magic of sharing your true self, should you choose to emulate Enice Toussaint's quiet grace.

Sincerely, Renata Martin, Author of the Ventures Series

Foreword

Why *a woman, amongst others*? Because it is a human story. An incredible tale, perhaps an ordinary one, however, as are being lived and have been lived by many women in the world. Why twelve lives? As a cat landing back on its paws... with an added three lives to its original nine.

This book is the first journal of written memoirs from 1989 to 1999 by Enice Toussaint, a bighearted, simple woman who got through the first fifty years of her life led by circumstances, meetings, travels, and also joys, always holding strong to faith and sense of family which has become scarce in our day and age.

It was in August 1999 when I first met Enice, accompanied by her daughter Natatsha, in a café on Côte-desNeiges. We talked about collaborating for the publication of her first book, and when the time came to hand me over her manuscript, filled with apprehension, she nevertheless handed me her treasure: two spiral notebooks filled with squeezed-up writing and ripened lined pages from being turned and turned. Immediately, I perceived in her gesture the sacredness and pain contained within these journals; this convinced me to collaborate in this project of publishing.

In the book's beginnings, we kept dated passages so as to acquaint ourselves with the text as it originally appeared within the two notebooks, in journal form of personal memory. I hope the readers will appreciate this tale of liberty, in all simplicity, as much as I appreciated reviewing it with its Author — perhaps a woman amongst others, one, however, who found a way to become herself and affirm her identity within its own self-defining truth.

Julie Martineau December 2001

Prologue

May 16, 1989

For as long as I can remember, I've thought about writing my life story. It was always a fleeting idea, something I wanted to do but never began. Now that my children have grown and I've started sharing bits of my life with them, their encouragement, especially from Max, has reignited that desire.

When I was a young girl, Sister Berthe gifted me a diary for my thirteenth birthday. That diary became a repository for my life experiences, starting from the time before my mama passed away to my eventual return from New York. Years later, my second husband read that diary and chose to burn it, claiming it was too filled with sadness. I tried to explain that it also held moments of joy, but the damage was done. His act left me feeling as though a part of me had been erased forever.

Even after that painful loss, the idea of writing my story lingered. I knew it wouldn't be easy, but it felt necessary—a way to reclaim and preserve those pieces of myself. Now, I am determined. I'll need luck and moments of solitude. And perhaps, a chance to escape into my own company for clarity and inspiration.

Saturday, April 27, 1997

This spring morning was unlike any other. I woke early in the convent where I've been staying for a month—a temporary refuge to reflect and find inner peace. Yet peace feels elusive, as though some unfamiliar part of myself is keeping me from truly being whole.

Seeking solace, I turned to my adopted mother, Sister Berthe of the Sœurs de la Sagesse, and asked her to help me find a retreat. Here, in this modest religious house, I hoped to feel closer to God, to seek his guidance as I navigated through the shadows of my life.

The morning began simply: I rose, showered, joined the others for breakfast, and participated in the Saturday Mass. During the service, I thanked God for the strength and grace that have carried me this far. Back in my room, a curious mix of joy and unease filled me. Sitting by the small window, I gazed out at the world below—a neighborhood alive with people, nature, and the quiet bustle of life.

The beauty of it all was overwhelming: the pure blue sky, trees poised to bloom, and the rhythmic hum of people living their lives. It was in this moment, as I observed the scene before me, that I felt a divine spark—a clarity. I realized that my story was ready to be written, not forced but allowed to flow naturally. Before I could move forward into the future, I needed to revisit the past one final time, to confront it, heal, and make peace.

May 3, 1997

Today, the weight of my memories was heavier than usual. I woke early, my stomach tight with unease. My thoughts lingered on the sadness that has marked my life—the pain of losing my mother and the countless struggles since. Each memory feels like a wound I'm reluctant to touch, yet I know I must.

Writing my story is a way of honoring my mama and, perhaps, a way of healing myself. The process feels daunting, but I am determined to persevere.

May 21, 2000

La Boule, Port-au-Prince

It is election day in Haiti, and the streets are eerily quiet. As a precaution, we stayed indoors. After hours of writing, I ventured into the courtyard, a serene space surrounded by flowers and trees, nestled against the backdrop of forested mountains and stately homes. It was like stepping into a dream—a moment of peace that felt almost sacred.

The blue sky stretched close, as though I could reach out and touch it, and I felt a deep sense of freedom. In this stillness, my thoughts came alive, and I felt a renewed purpose. Writing and living are intertwined, and in this moment, I felt capable of embracing both.

1

First Life

A Happy Childhood

With My Family in Miragoâne, Haiti

As a child, I had an imaginary friend. She wasn't just a playmate but someone I trusted deeply, confiding in her whenever I faced problems. She always seemed to have the answers, guiding me when I needed direction. Back then, I believed she was my guardian angel. Now, as an adult, she remains a constant presence. She has aged with me and continues to offer advice. When I resist her counsel, she becomes displeased, leading me to suspect she might be another version of myself—a part of me I have yet to fully understand.

Breaking through the wall within myself feels like an impossible task. Each attempt leaves me blocked, but I know I must try. This division, this split in my soul, needs healing.

My Mother and Our Family

My mother, Estelle, was born into a respectable family in a village near Miragoâne. She was a devoted woman with a strong character and a generous heart. Despite limited education, she raised six children—three boys and three girls—ensuring we grew up in a loving and disciplined household.

When she met my father, he already had three children with other women. Yet my mother, principled and steadfast, refused to give herself to him unless they were married. My father, a charming ladies' man, obliged. After their marriage, my mother insisted that his children from previous relationships, particularly a young girl named Claire, receive a proper education and be brought to live with us.

My mother was a woman of many talents—a seamstress, a merchant, and above all, a nurturer. She took our studies seriously, often meeting with our headmistress, Sister Berthe, to discuss our progress. She cared for the poor, welcomed them to our home every Saturday for food and clothes, and treated our household staff with kindness and respect, considering them part of the family.

She was also deeply spiritual. Our home had a small chapel where we prayed together every evening. Her faith and love extended equally to all her children, biological and otherwise. We never wanted for anything while she was alive, and her absence remains a profound loss.

My Father

My father, Frantz, was a striking figure—handsome, well-groomed, and witty. He came from a large family and was well-educated, a rarity at the time. Though he had a playful nature and loved to pamper us, he was also a traditional Haitian man, deeply rooted in the patriarchal norms of our society.

He made his living traveling from city to city, often absent during the day but bringing joy and indulgence when he returned home at night. My mother frequently chastised him for spoiling us and ignoring our mischief, but he always responded with a smile, saying, ―Let them be; I don't see them often.‖

Though my parents rarely argued in front of us, my father's wandering eyes often tested my mother's patience. In Haiti, many men father children with multiple women, a cultural norm that causes silent suffering among wives. My father was no exception, but he loved us in his way, ensuring we grew up in a secure and prosperous environment.

Our Home in Miragoâne

We lived in two family homes, both brimming with life and love. The first, located on Grande-Rue, was a small but charming house with a shop in front and a backyard filled with plants and a fragrant white camellia tree. It was here that we studied, played, and shared countless memories.

The second house was more spacious, featuring a high balcony, beautifully crafted mahogany furniture, and a large mirror in the living room that I adored. Both homes reflected my parents' hard work and devotion to providing for us. They were places of comfort and joy, where even the smallest details, like the pigeons in the backyard or the neighbors' voices over the fence, became part of our story.

Reflections

Looking back, my childhood in Miragoâne was a tapestry of love, discipline, and resilience. My mother's unwavering strength and my father's lighthearted spirit shaped our family in profound ways. Despite the challenges, we were a close-knit unit, bound by faith, tradition, and a deep sense of belonging.

My journey now involves piecing together these memories, understanding the roles they played in shaping who I am, and reconciling the divides within myself. It's a daunting task, but one I approach with hope and determination.

Irène, Robert, and Me

I was born on October 1st, at 10 o'clock in the morning—a small, frail baby with light skin, brown eyes, and curly hair. My parents had hoped for a boy, especially my mother, as they already had a little girl, Irène. Yet they welcomed me with love, a sentiment that never wavered, especially after they had two sons, Robert and Julien. Tragically, Julien passed away at just two years old.

Growing up, I was told I was a thin and sickly child. My family often recounted the day I fainted for so long that my mother thought I had died. Despite these challenges, I was a sensitive, shy, and often tearful little girl who loved laughter and play. My sister Irène, always studious and serious, protected me fiercely, and my younger brother Robert became my closest companion. Together, we were inseparable, sharing a bond that grew deeper as we played and laughed through childhood.

I often found myself drawn to the games Robert and his friends played. One afternoon, while playing with them, I stepped on a screw that lodged deep into my foot. Initially, I felt no pain and continued on, but the situation worsened when my mother noticed blood gushing from my foot. Her panic brought everyone running, including neighbors, and a doctor was called to stop the bleeding. Though the crisis passed, my mother scolded me afterward, saying, ―You should be playing with dolls, not with boys.‖ Yet her words were quickly forgotten, and I returned to my beloved games.

Our Childhood Games and Bond

I loved playing mother and father, skipping rope, running, playing hide-and-seek, and even building toy cars with Robert. These games were our escape, filling our days with joy and laughter. Singing was another love of mine—I often hummed melodies, even when I didn't know the lyrics. My happiness was contagious, and despite my frailty, I was the heart of our playful moments.

Irène, though not one to join our games, was a pillar of love and protection. Our separation after Mama's death was an especially painful wound. She was my guide, my protector, and my steady force during those formative years.

Robert, being younger, was my constant shadow. Together, we navigated the small adventures of our childhood, forming a bond that weathered every storm. My other siblings, much older, were figures of respect in our household, a value deeply ingrained in Haitian family traditions.

Sweet Memories

Sugar was my weakness. My mother, a merchant, often bought sweets in bulk to resell, and I would tuck some under my pillow each night. My older sister Claire, always watchful, would find and take them away, much to my dismay. On nights when I overindulged, I convinced myself that eating something salty would prevent diabetes—a child's logic to ease her conscience.

Bedtime was always a tender moment. Claire would sing lullabies to soothe me to sleep, her gentle voice weaving dreams into the night:

—*Dodo ti pitit manman, si ou pa dodo, krab-la va manje-w. Dodo pitit, krab nan calalou*‖ (Sleep, mommy's little girl; if you don't sleep, the crab will eat you. Sleep, my little one, the crab is in the calalou).

Being the fragile child in the family, I was often spoiled with my favorite foods—chicken, rice, ice cream, and sweets. My mother's love and indulgence left me feeling cherished, even as I struggled with my health.

Reflection

Looking back, my childhood was a blend of laughter, love, and resilience. Despite the hardships, the bonds I shared with my siblings, particularly Robert and Irène, were unbreakable. These moments, filled with both sweetness and sorrow, shaped me into the person I am today. They remain a testament to the enduring strength of family and the simple joys of childhood.

In School

My first day of school is a memory etched with both fear and excitement. My mother accompanied Irène and me, ensuring we were settled. Afterward, Claire, my older sister, took over the responsibility of waking us at 5:30 every morning. Though early, it allowed us enough time to wash, eat breakfast, and prepare for the day ahead. A servant would bathe and dress us, while Claire handled our hair. This was often a source of tension, as I disliked the little braids she insisted on making. I preferred my hair loose with a large bow on my forehead—a look reserved for Sundays, church, or special occasions. During the week, however, I endured the braids, even though I tried my best to avoid them.

Each school morning began at 7:00 a.m., with classes starting an hour later. Initially, I struggled to adapt. On the very first day, I clung to Irène, crying uncontrollably when my mother left. The nuns, understanding my distress, allowed me to sit in Irène's class for the first week until I found my footing. Once I made friends, my fears dissipated, and school became a place of joy and discovery.

The Journey to and from School

Our school, Notre-Dame de Lourdes, run by the Sœurs de la Sagesse, was located in the city's upper part, on Bel-Air Street. The journey from our home on Grande-Rue to the school was both an adventure and a challenge. Each day, I walked down Bel-Air Street, passing the church where I faithfully made the sign of the cross, climbed a large staircase, and arrived home by lunchtime.

As I grew older, my friends and I would turn this journey into a race, dashing down Bel-Air Street and up the staircase with boundless energy. My mother's friend, who lived near the staircase, often warned her about our reckless running, saying, ―One of these days, she'll hurt herself!‖ My mother's scoldings temporarily curbed my enthusiasm, but soon enough, I was back to my playful antics.

School Life and Memories

The school itself was a vibrant place. Kindergarten classes were held under a large, metal-roofed tent, while the elementary school stood nearby. Recess was a time of laughter and games in the shade of tall trees. During the hottest days, school hours were reduced to half-days, and the rain often brought unexpected holidays. Despite school closures, children still gathered to play, and I was no exception.

In kindergarten and first grade, I was taught by nuns who left a lasting impression on me. One of my favorite teachers, Mademoiselle Martine, stood out for her elegance and poise. Her impeccable appearance and dignified demeanor captivated us. My friends and I often imitated her mannerisms in our secret hideouts, dreaming of becoming as graceful as her. In many ways, I aspired to emulate her, though her austerity was a quality I never quite adopted.

Reflections

My school years were marked by growth, both academically and personally. From the nervous tears of my first day to the confidence gained through friendships and play, those early experiences shaped my character. The influence of inspiring figures like Mademoiselle Martine, coupled with the daily rituals of school life, instilled in me a sense of discipline and a love for learning. These memories remain a cherished part of my journey.

Nounoune and Holidays

I have always cherished my nickname, —Nounoune,‖ given to me by my father. It became a term of endearment that my family often used, especially during joyful moments. My brother Alain, however, had a different nickname for me——Bout fè,‖ or —piece of iron.‖ This stemmed from my childhood, when I was thin, energetic, and hard-playing, often wearing out my clothes and shoes. Alain would joke that I was as tough as a piece of iron, a name that still lingers.

Christmas Traditions

Childhood Christmases were magical in our household. My father often traveled to Port-au-Prince to purchase merchandise for my mother's store, bringing back an abundance of toys and gifts. The excitement began a month before Christmas with a unique tradition: merchants would organize lotteries. My mother and sister Claire participated, setting up a table on our balcony covered with numbered items like toys and trinkets. Customers would draw numbers for a chance to win. I loved the lively atmosphere, the ringing bell, and the festive cheer.

Christmas in our home came with a stipulation: good grades. My parents would warn us, especially my brother and me, that poor school performance meant no gifts. Yet, no matter how our grades turned out, we always found presents at the foot of our beds on Christmas morning. My mother would say, "Santa Claus said it's not too bad this year, but next year, you'll have to do better."

One unforgettable Christmas at school involved Santa Claus himself. Sister Berthe's brother, visiting from Canada, dressed as Santa and handed out gifts. The sight of him in his red suit and booming "Ho! Ho! Ho!" left us awestruck. We sang "Petit papa Noël" and lined up to receive our presents. That moment cemented my belief in the magic of Christmas, a sentiment I carry to this day. My husband often teases me about how I act like a child during the holidays, but I embrace the joy and wonder of the season.

New Year's Day Celebrations

New Year's Day was another cherished holiday in Haiti. Preparations began weeks in advance with houses being repainted and cleaned. On New Year's Eve, families engaged in a thorough, all-night cleaning to welcome the new year with a sparkling home. Morning traditions included coffee and giraumont, with neighbors exchanging dishes. The day was filled with cake, strong liqueur, and laughter as children, dressed in new clothes, visited homes to share New Year's wishes and receive treats.

January 2, in contrast, was an adult-focused celebration featuring turkey and quieter gatherings. While the festivities marked renewal and hope, they also deepened community bonds through shared traditions and generosity.

A Less Joyous Holiday: Mardi Gras

While Christmas and New Year's brought joy, Mardi Gras was a season of fear for me. Each Sunday, a sense of dread overcame me as the festival approached. I would hide under the bed, heart pounding, unable to shake the unease. The vibrant celebrations, so loved by others, left me anxious and uneasy.

Reflections

The holidays of my childhood were a blend of joy, tradition, and occasional trepidation. From the warmth of family gatherings to the magic of Christmas and the unity of New Year's, these moments remain etched in my memory. Even the more challenging experiences, like my fear of Mardi Gras, shaped the tapestry of my childhood. They remind me of the importance of preserving traditions and the beauty of shared celebrations, no matter how they evolve over time.

Mother's Death

> *"Do not be sad over what you have lost.*
> *Be grateful to have had it."*
> *– Saint Augustine*

In 1956, my mother was pregnant, and our household buzzed with excitement. My siblings—Irène, Robert, and I—eagerly awaited the baby's arrival. The idea of having a new sibling filled our hearts with joy. Yet, amidst this happiness, a shadow loomed. My father began an affair with a much younger woman, the sister of one of my mother's close friends. Naively, my mother remained unaware of this betrayal, even welcoming the woman into our home under the guise of friendship. Little did she know, this woman, Vanité, sought to take her place in every sense, even resorting to harmful practices like magic to eliminate my mother.

The last day I spent with my mother was a spring Sunday in May—Mother's Day in Haiti. We had given her a gift that morning, and she was radiant with joy. I played with her beautiful wavy hair, curling it gently at her request, happy just to be close to her. Yet, I now realize she must have known her time was near. At one point, she remarked, "Look at how white my hands and skin are. Don't you think it's because I don't have much blood left?" Though her words hinted at the hemorrhaging she had been enduring, those around her dismissed it lightly. I was too young to understand the gravity of her condition.

Her Final Hours

That evening, my mother's health took a turn for the worse, and she was rushed to Paillant Hospital. By nightfall, the decision was made to transfer her to Port-au-Prince for specialized care. Before leaving, she gave my sister Claire instructions about money and reminded the neighbors to watch over us. Her final words to my brother and me were filled with love and wisdom, urging us to be kind and good to others. Even as she left, I clung to the hope that she would return with our baby sibling.

As we lay in bed that night, a persistent fly buzzed around the room, keeping us awake—a strange and unsettling detail that remains vivid in my memory. The next morning, I went to school dressed in my Girl Scout uniform, preparing for a celebration. Yet, my mind was consumed with thoughts of Mama.

The News

Around 10 a.m., someone arrived at school to deliver the devastating news. I was called to the principal's office, where

Sister Berthe gently broke it to me: my mother had passed away. Walking home, I noticed the somber faces and muffled cries of neighbors. The realization hit me like a tidal wave—Mama was gone forever.

Unlike my sister Irène, who openly wept and wailed, I was struck silent by the weight of my grief. I couldn't cry or scream; the pain was too overwhelming. As the house filled with mourners, I felt detached, as though I were living in another world. That day marked the end of my first life, a turning point after which nothing was ever the same.

Unspoken Fears

In the days leading up to her death, there had been signs—omens, perhaps—that hinted at the tragic outcome. One Saturday, as we worked in my mother's shop, a peculiar object fell near her. It was a bundle of pins, hot peppers, and other items associated with curses. My mother ordered it thrown away and forbade anyone from mentioning it to my father. From that day, her health began to decline.

She confided in a neighbor about recurring nightmares of a beast tearing at her abdomen. The neighbor's reassurances of faith couldn't shield her from the growing darkness. Reflecting on these events later, I came to understand the forces working against her, both physical and spiritual.

Legacy of Loss

My mother's death was a profound loss that altered the course of my life. Her strength, kindness, and love remain etched in my memory. Even in her final moments, she thought of her children and imparted lessons that continue to guide me. The pain of losing her will never fade, but her legacy endures in the values she instilled in us.

Death

"Why death? Death, the unacceptable, which we must learn to accept."

Death is an undeniable reality, yet it feels unbearable. It exists around us and within us, a force that inevitably takes away what we hold most dear. We must not deceive ourselves into believing we are safe from its reach. It will come, leaving scars that remain vivid and alive, marking us forever. And yet, in the shadow of death, we must find a way to live.

The death of a loved one feels like a cyclone, pulling you into its chaos, threatening to drown you in sorrow. But we cannot allow ourselves to remain trapped. Survival is not just a necessity but an act of faithfulness to those who have passed. Locking ourselves in grief dishonors their memory. Instead, we must strive to live as they would have lived—to continue the journey they can no longer walk.

To honor the departed, we must keep their essence alive within us. We must carry their faces, voices, and thoughts into the future, passing them down to others. Through us, their shortened lives can bear perpetual fruit, creating a legacy that outlasts the pain of their absence.

2

Second life

After Mama's Death

My Friends and Adolescence

I was a fragile and naïve little girl who grew into a strong-willed yet sensitive adolescent. My innocence and fearfulness lingered as I spent much of my time with my brother Robert and his friends, who were mostly boys. Among them was Sylvain, who had feelings for me. Though I could have reciprocated, I was too young and unprepared for such emotions.

Among my few close female friends was Violette, my godmother Ruth's daughter. Our friendship faded after a conflict, leaving us estranged for years. In contrast, Doris was like a sister to me. She stepped into the role of playmate that my studious sister Irène never filled. Doris and I were inseparable—until one event shattered my trust in her.

Doris was full of life, playful, and far more open-minded than I was. I, vulnerable and impressionable, followed her lead unquestioningly. Once, during a sleepover at her house, Doris attempted to kiss me. Stunned, I let her for a brief moment before pulling away. She tried to convince me it was normal between friends, but I resisted, relieved when others in the room interrupted her persistence. From that day on, I vowed never to share a bed with another friend, a promise I kept.

Though our friendship continued briefly, my perception of Doris was forever altered. She often led me into trouble, including sneaking off to the countryside without informing anyone. This escapade earned me two thorough scoldings from my sisters. Doris moved to Port-au-Prince when we were 11, and though our friendship ended, the lessons from those years stayed with me. My trusting nature often left me vulnerable to influence, a trait that shaped many of my experiences.

Life After Mama's Death

After my mother's passing, my childhood home became a shadow of what it once was. My sister Claire, whom we called ―Ma Tante‖ out of respect, took care of us until her marriage. My father, now living with his mistress Vanité, rarely visited, leaving us in the care of a servant and our mother's friend, Aunt Dieula.

Aunt Dieula, a strong and religious woman, became our lifeline. She owned a bakery and provided us with bread and supplies weekly, ensuring we had enough to eat. Despite her stern demeanor, she had a generous heart and often entertained us with stories. She was a complex figure—unforgiving of those who crossed her but fiercely protective of those she cared for.

My father's absence deepened our struggles. Though Mama had left money and goods for us, they mysteriously disappeared. Her business and possessions vanished as well. The void she left was filled with sadness and longing. My father's decision to move Vanité into Mama's house only fueled my resentment toward him, a bitterness I carried for years.

When my father fell ill, he asked to see me. Reluctantly, I visited him. His whispered plea for forgiveness softened my anger. I kissed him, granting the forgiveness he sought. He passed away shortly after, and with his death, a heavy burden lifted from my heart.

A New Chapter

After my father's death, my siblings and I were scattered. Irène moved to Port-au-Prince to continue her studies, Robert went to live with our uncle Joseph, and I stayed with Aunt Dieula to finish grade school. These separations were painful, yet they underscored the importance of education—a value my mother had instilled in us.

Eventually, my mother's sister, Anna, brought me to Port-au-Prince to continue my education. She promised we would reunite with Robert, and though her intentions may not have been purely selfless, I was overjoyed to leave for the capital. With an orphan's heart, I clung to the hope of finding a semblance of family and comfort in this new chapter of my life.

3

Third Life

Aunt Anna's House

A Difficult Year

Living at Aunt Anna's house in Port-au-Prince was a profoundly unhappy experience. Her home was cramped, with one large room divided by a folding screen. While her children—Suzie and her two sons—slept in a bed, we were relegated to the floor. I was terrified of sleeping there, yet I had no choice. Aunt Dieula had generously sent provisions and money for my brother's and my schooling, but Aunt Anna used these resources for her own children, leaving us with crumbs. She cooked meals in two batches: one for her children with the best of the supplies, and another with leftovers for us. Even the money intended for our education was spent on her children's schooling, clothing, and shoes.

When Aunt Anna moved to a bigger house, my hopes of finally having a bed to sleep in were dashed. Instead, she announced she was taking in tenants and we would continue sleeping on the living room floor. One evening, she told me that if I wanted to sleep in a bed, I would have to share it with one of the boarders and ―do everything he asked of me.‖ Horrified, I refused, declaring, ―I came here for school, not for this. I would rather sleep on the floor—or die.‖ Furious, she condemned me back to the floor, where bitterness and despair became my constant companions.

A Betrayal Uncovered

Days turned into weeks, and I noticed that while other children went to school, I remained at home. Each time I asked Aunt Anna when I would start school, she brushed me off with vague promises of ―tomorrow.‖ Finally, she announced that she would take me to enroll. Suzie escorted me to the principal's office, but when I entered, I realized the horrifying truth: my aunt expected me to prostitute myself to secure a place at the school.

In shock, I ran back to Aunt Anna's house, only to be met with a slap from Suzie. She tried to force me to return, but I refused. Overwhelmed with sadness and anger, I fled to Madame Médé, Aunt Dadia's mother, and poured out my story. Suzie followed to fetch me, but when Aunt Anna arrived, I clung to the stairway handrail, enduring a beating from her piece of wood without letting go. Exhausted, she finally gave up, and I seized the moment to tell her, ―I'm leaving for Miragoâne.‖

The Journey Home

The next day, accompanied by Aunt Anna, I made my way to the train station with my brother Robert. But he fled in fear, seeking refuge with Uncle Joseph. Alone, I returned to Miragoâne with Aunt Anna and went straight to my sister Claire's house, hoping for help. To my dismay, Claire refused to let me stay, angrily insisting that I return to Port-au-Prince with Aunt Anna.

Heartbroken, I sought out Aunt Dieula, the one person I knew would care for me. She welcomed me with open arms, bathed and fed me, and offered me the safety I so desperately needed. That night, as I lay in bed, my troubles momentarily faded. I had found solace with someone who treated me like her own.

Confrontation and Resolution

The following day, Claire and Aunt Anna arrived to take me back to Port-au-Prince. However, Aunt Dieula stood firm. —Enice is staying with me, she declared. —Are you not ashamed after all that Enice's mother did for you? You would have her return to Port-au-Prince to prostitute herself? I am ashamed of you, Claire.

She then turned to Aunt Anna, demanding, —Return the money I sent for Enice and Robert's education. She is thin and has told me about the way you've treated her. How could you do this to your own sister's children? With no money left, Aunt Anna was forced to accept additional funds from Aunt Dieula to return to Port-au-Prince. For the first time in months, I felt a sense of justice and relief.

Reflections

The year I spent with Aunt Anna was one of the most difficult periods of my life. It taught me about betrayal and resilience, the cruelty of those who should protect us, and the kindness of those who truly care. Though the scars of that time remain, the unwavering support of Aunt Dieula reminded me that even in the darkest moments, love and compassion can prevail.

4

Fourth life

Return to Miragoâne

At Aunt Dieula's Home

Returning to Aunt Dieula's house in Miragoâne was a relief compared to the previous years of hardship. Life there wasn't ideal, but it was tolerable, especially since no one else wanted us. Shortly after my arrival, my sister Irène, who had been studying nursing in Cayes, fell ill. Naturally, she turned to Aunt Dieula for help. True to her character, Aunt Dieula paid for my sister's medical care, and once Irène recovered, she stayed with us for a few months before moving to Port-au-Prince to live with another aunt, one of my father's sisters.

Aunt Dieula's home was modest, reflecting her simple way of living, which we respected. She was strict and had a strong personality, often speaking her mind regardless of who was around. Despite her sternness, I appreciated her care and the sense of stability she provided. I began attending Mont-Rose College, a mixed school—a new and exciting experience for me. Though I enjoyed my time there, my friendships were short-lived as I did not return the following year.

First Love

It was during this time that I met Henry, a young man who came to Miragoâne for the summer holidays to visit his mother. He was shy but charming, and though we barely spoke, we shared a mutual affection. Each time I passed his house, he would follow me silently, managing only a polite ―hello.‖ My responses were equally timid, as if my voice was caught in my throat.

Our communication blossomed through letters, delivered by a neighbor girl who became our secret messenger. This innocent courtship continued throughout the summer until Henry returned to Port-au-Prince. Though brief, our connection left a lasting impression on my heart.

A Dream That Changed Everything

Before the summer ended, my brother Alain invited me to live with him, promising a better life. He had recently married and moved into our late mother's house, furnishing it with her belongings and using her wedding ring to bless his marriage. Initially, I spent my days at his house and nights at Aunt Dieula's, but Alain insisted I move in fully, assuring me that his presence would protect me.

From the beginning, it was clear that Alain's wife resented my presence. She refused to let me eat at the table when Alain wasn't home, criticized everything I did, and often fabricated stories to turn him against me. One evening, after another of her lies, Alain confronted me, accusing me of inappropriate behavior. Despite my denials, he lost his temper and began beating me while his wife goaded him on. Her spiteful laughter and his harsh blows were unbearable, yet I stayed silent, determined not to give her the satisfaction of seeing me cry.

That night, after the punishment ended, I lay on the floor, overwhelmed with despair. I called out to my mother in my heart, pleading for her to take me away from this misery. As I drifted into an exhausted sleep, I had a dream that felt more real than reality itself. My mother appeared, dressed in a beautiful pink dress adorned with white flowers. She gestured for me to follow her, leading me to a large house. Though she did not enter with me, her smile and presence filled me with peace.

A New Beginning

The dream filled me with an unexplainable strength. I woke early the next morning, determined to leave. Quietly, I packed my belongings and slipped out of the house before anyone else was awake. My destination was clear: Sister Berthe's home. When I arrived at my sister's friend's house, I announced my intention. Though surprised, they supported my decision.

Later that day, after attending mass, I approached Sister Berthe, declaring, —I've come to you because I can no longer endure my life as it is. I need your help." She embraced me warmly and replied, —"I've been waiting for you." Her words reassured me, and I felt an overwhelming sense of safety and hope. With Sister Berthe's promise to take care of me, my sister left in tears, and I entered a new chapter of my life at the nun's boarding school.

5

Fifth life

With the Nuns

My Arrival at the Convent

The day I arrived at the sisters' convent, I felt an overwhelming sense of happiness. It was as if I had finally found a place where I belonged. For the first time in years, I felt at peace, unburdened by the struggles I had left behind. It was the summer of 1962, and the school was on break, so there were no boarders. One of the nuns gave me a tour of the convent, a large and serene place. When I reached the dormitory, memories of the dream I had at my brother Alain's house flooded back. I thought to myself, —Mama led me here. I had asked her to come and get me, and she heard me. Instead of taking me with her, she brought me to the nuns. This is her final gift to me.‖

Some people might dismiss dreams as meaningless, but I believe in their power. That dream had given me strength, and now I understood it was meant to guide me here.

Rediscovering Joy

Sister Berthe made it her mission to help me rediscover joy. She was adamant that I should not dwell in sadness, and from the very first day, she gently encouraged me to smile again. I hadn't smiled since my mother's death, but Sister Berthe's warmth and persistent kindness began to heal me. Whenever she saw me lost in sorrow, she would smile at me until I smiled back. Gradually, her method worked, and I found myself wanting to smile again, to embrace life.

A Beacon of Light

It's hard to put into words the profound impact Sister Berthe had on my life. A Canadian by origin, she belonged to the congregation of *Les Sœurs de la Sagesse*. She had come to Port-au-Prince as a young nun and was later transferred to Miragoâne, where she became the headmistress of the school. To me, she was like a ray of sunshine—so graceful and radiant that she seemed otherworldly. She carried herself with an elegance that captivated everyone, especially when she wore her habit. Her soft voice and gentle smile brought comfort to all who met her.

As a child, I used to think that nuns were untouchable, immune to the ordinary sensations of life. I believed they didn't even feel pain—until the day one of them punished me by making me kneel in front of the blackboard. Curious, I used a pin to prick her, expecting no reaction. She flinched slightly and brushed at the spot, thinking it was a bug. That moment shattered my childish illusion; they were human after all.

A Safe Haven

Living under Sister Berthe's care, I discovered a side of her that went beyond the strictness required to manage the school. At the convent, she revealed her true nature—a kind and compassionate woman with a heart full of love. She became my protector, mentor, and a source of comfort. For the first time since my mother's passing, I felt safe and cherished. The convent wasn't just a place of refuge; it became my home.

The City of Miragoâne

The nuns' house stood as a grand yellow structure, clean and inviting, on Bel-Air Street in the city's upper part, offering a picturesque view of Miragoâne. During the 1960s, Miragoâne was a small but stunning city, marked by its unique blend of natural and architectural beauty.

Miragoâne was divided into two distinct parts: the lower city, nestled in a crevasse as if reclaimed from the sea, and the upper city, perched on the mountain, overlooking the ocean. This geographical juxtaposition enhanced the city's allure, creating a breathtaking panorama.

Upon entering the city from Port-au-Prince, travelers passed through Léogâne, Grand-Goâve, Petit-Goâve, and then reached

Desruisseaux, the gateway to Miragoâne. This bustling crossroad was alive with activity. Vendors lined the streets with food and wares, competing for the attention of travelers. It was a colorful chaos, where small, informal restaurants coexisted with vendors of fried bananas, pork, and sweet potatoes. The aroma of freshly fried delicacies filled the air, mingling with the energy of the crowd.

In the upper city, Bel-Air Street was a notable landmark. The Saint-Jean-Baptiste Church, a striking architectural masterpiece, stood tall on a rocky hill. To reach the church, visitors ascended steep staircases that led to a serene grotto featuring a statue of Our Lady of Lourdes and cascading water droplets. From the church's vantage point, one could marvel at the lower city and the vast blue ocean, with the island of Gonâve visible on the horizon.

The lower city, known as Bas-Fort, was home to markets, small shops, and residential areas. Grande-Rue, the main street, housed important institutions like the police headquarters and Téléco, along with general stores and a pharmacy. The heart of the city was La Place, a communal square featuring a fountain and a charming statue of a little boy who watered the surrounding flowers. It was a popular spot for social gatherings and a cherished memory from my childhood.

Miragoâne also had its share of historical significance. The Reynolds aluminum company once thrived in the area, leaving behind remnants of its operations, including large, abandoned buildings. Nearby, Source-Salée Street derived its name from a lightly salted freshwater spring. The street was home to quaint houses, a school, and a Protestant church.

The city's charm extended to Nouvelle Cité, where my father had his speculator's office and where he and his friend Madame Légère once invested in properties. This part of the city, with its lush green mountains and cool climate, provided a tranquil retreat from the bustling lower city.

Miragoâne, with its distinct districts and cultural richness, was my paradise. Although time has changed its landscape, the memories of its serene beaches, vibrant streets, and peaceful mountain retreats remain vivid. It was more than a city; it was the heart of my childhood, a place of beauty and innocence that shaped the foundation of who I am.

My Life with the Sisters

The Sisters' residence was a sanctuary of comfort and structure. The first floor housed a spacious dormitory for employees, a grand dining hall for the Sisters, and a separate dining area for boarders and staff. Bathrooms were conveniently located on the balcony. Upstairs, there was the headmistress's office and a large communal space for the nuns, furnished with a piano, sewing machines, and a game table. Adjacent to the headmistress's office, a small shop offered school supplies to students.

Five classrooms surrounded the grounds, one of which doubled as a theater for school performances. The third floor featured the Sisters' private quarters, linen closets, bathrooms, and the boarders' dormitory. The dormitory's design was thoughtful: four large rooms, each equipped with three small beds, and a hallway that opened to breathtaking views of the city and its surroundings. From there, we could observe the boys in the neighborhood strumming guitars, trying to catch the attention of the boarders—a harmless mischief that amused us but displeased the nuns.

The exterior of the residence was equally captivating. Rows of vibrant roses, especially the yellow ones I adored, framed the building. A prominent statue of Our Lady of Lourdes stood near the entrance, with a grand staircase leading to the main gate. A long cement pathway, lined with laurel trees and a grapevine-covered terrace, offered a peaceful retreat. This was my favorite spot, where I could watch the bustling city, converse with neighbors, or simply reflect.

To the left of the pathway lay the food warehouse, a state-of-the-art kitchen for the Sisters, and a coal kitchen alongside a pastry classroom. The yard also had a washhouse and an exit leading to the school's other half. This exit opened to the generator room, the chaplain's modest house, and a beautiful chapel where we attended mass. Beyond the chapel, a wide alley connected to the school's playground and elementary classrooms, which were uniquely built on pile foundations. Beneath these classrooms, shaded areas served as study and play zones for students.

The chapel's priest, Father Devos, lived in a nearby house that offered stunning views of Cérôme, the ocean, and the island of La Gonâve. Watching the ships sail by was a calming and inspiring experience, one that I cherished deeply.

Amédé, the gatekeeper, was a kind man who often acted as my messenger. Walking further along the path behind the elementary classrooms, one would find a long garden and storage spaces beneath the classrooms. This path eventually circled back to the washhouse near the main building.

These surroundings became more than just a place of learning and discipline; they represented a chapter of healing and rediscovery. My time here, amidst the Sisters' care, marked one of the most beautiful and transformative periods of my life.

Growing Up with the Nuns

Childhood for me was the most challenging period of my life. Losing my mother plunged me into a series of hardships that seemed endless. Yet, despite the pain, I trusted God and held onto the belief that my mother was watching over me. I often wished to join her in heaven to escape the anguish. However, when I began living with the nuns, life slowly started to feel less burdensome.

That summer marked the first time since my mother's death that I felt a semblance of happiness. It was as if I had been liberated from my sorrows. With no family present, my mind focused only on the present—no thoughts of my sister Irène or my brother Robert. It all felt like a dream. The nuns' convent was my sanctuary, a place where I believed no further troubles could reach me.

During the holidays, I stayed in the employees' dormitory on the first floor, as the boarders had not yet returned. This arrangement suited me well; after the traumatic events I had endured, I felt safer sleeping near others. Each evening, the employees gathered to socialize after dinner. We would greet Sister Berthe and the other nuns as they left the dining hall, then retreat to the recreation room to unwind. These routines brought me a sense of normalcy.

Sister Berthe, the headmistress, introduced me to the employees and spoke to them about my situation. She asked them to care for me, and they welcomed me warmly. Among them were five young women and a man named Amédé, who became a trusted friend and messenger. Jeanette, the youngest, later joined the nuns, a decision that inspired me. Their tasks included cooking, housekeeping, and maintaining the convent grounds. Despite their busy schedules, they made an effort to make me feel at home.

That first night, I was given a proper bed, a nightstand, and a small dresser. Exhausted from the emotional toll of recent days, I fell asleep almost immediately. The next morning, I attended mass and spent time in prayer, thanking God, the Virgin Mary, and my mother for guiding me to this safe haven. After breakfast, Sister Berthe invited me to her office to outline my responsibilities during the holidays and what I could expect once school resumed.

My tasks were varied and engaging. I assisted Sister Marie-Marthe with cleaning the chapel, making small repairs, and painting around the convent. She worked with incredible dedication, and I learned a great deal from her. Additionally, I had the privilege of cleaning Sister Berthe's room, a task I treasured since it signified her trust in me. My days also included lessons in cooking and typing. In the afternoons, I enjoyed reading in the peaceful garden, surrounded by greenery and the distant sound of the ocean.

While the employees became my newfound family, I kept to myself when it came to my relatives. Aside from a visit from my sister Irène, who informed me she was leaving for Port-au-Prince, I had no contact with family members. My brother Robert was still in the capital, and my older sister Claire did not visit me. Surprisingly, I didn't feel their absence acutely. The peace I experienced with the nuns filled the void.

When October arrived, so did my birthday. To my delight, Sister Berthe gave me a gift and suggested I visit family in town. I chose to visit my Aunt Dieula, who welcomed me warmly and even gave me a small gift. Later that day, I returned to the convent, content and excited to begin school and move into the dormitory on the third floor. For the first time, I felt proud of my place in the world.

With the return of the boarders, my life became more structured. Discipline was strict but necessary. Mornings began at 5 a.m. with Sister Jean waking us up with a cheerful —Blessed be our Lord Jesus Christ,‖ to which we responded, —Through Mary.‖ Each day followed a precise routine: prayer, classes, meals, and supervised study sessions. Meals were a communal affair, often accompanied by Bible readings, and despite the occasional unappetizing dish, we learned the value of gratitude.

I formed close bonds with four fellow boarders: Colette, Joséphine, Miche, and Maguy. Together, we created a strong sense of camaraderie, often communicating in sign language during meals and sharing stories after lights-out. Although our late-night escapades sometimes led to punishment, they also strengthened our friendships.

Throughout my time at the convent, I found solace in prayer and the chapel. It became a sacred space where I felt closer to my mother and God. One day, I confessed to Sister Berthe my desire to become a nun. Her response was gentle and wise: —You are young and have endured so much. Take the time to live and pray. If you have the calling, it will come naturally.‖

Looking back, those years with the nuns were some of the most formative of my life. Despite the strict discipline, I felt loved, protected, and surrounded by a sense of purpose. It was a chapter of healing, one that allowed me to rediscover happiness and begin building a brighter future.

An Unexpected Encounter

Sister Berthe's transfer to the Notre-Dame-du-Sacré-Cœur school in Port-au-Prince brought immense sorrow to me. Her departure marked the beginning of a challenging period. Before leaving, she promised that I could spend the holidays in Port-au-Prince with the sisters at Saint-Joseph.

The difficult time began in late June during the Saint-Jean-Baptiste festival when the Frères du Sacré-Cœur blessed the first stone of their new school. After the ceremony, I headed back to the sisters' house, wearing a yellow dress with white polka dots that made me feel radiant. I was excited about the holidays and the chance to see Sister Berthe again.

As I passed one of the classrooms, a voice called out to me. Initially, I ignored it, but the voice was persistent. Reluctantly, I stopped. A man introduced himself as Tony Legros, an elementary school teacher at the brothers' school. He professed his love for me, asking if I would go out with him. I firmly rejected him, saying, ―No, I don't love you and never will.‖ Undeterred, he confidently claimed, ―I will marry you, and you will be my wife.‖ I retorted, ―Never, because I love someone else.‖

Tony's persistence extended to visiting the sisters and writing to them, proclaiming his intentions to marry me. The headmistress in

Miragoâne asked me about him, and I reiterated my disinterest, emphasizing my focus on the upcoming holidays.

That summer, I was delighted to leave for Port-au-Prince. In addition to seeing Sister Berthe, I could reconnect with my siblings, Robert and Irène. My father's sister, Aunt Dadia, also lived in the capital. A vivacious and sophisticated woman, Aunt Dadia had been part of my life since childhood. Despite her strong personality, we had a respectful and harmonious relationship.

Upon my arrival, Sister Berthe informed me of Tony's letter requesting my hand in marriage. I explained that I had no interest in marriage at the time, especially not with Tony. During the same summer, I learned my brother Robert had tuberculosis due to malnourishment. Sister Berthe's generosity extended to arranging his treatment and care, ensuring he had a safe place to recover.

While in Port-au-Prince, I encountered a young woman named Marie begging at Saint-Joseph church. She confided in me about her struggles, and my heart went out to her. I turned to Sister Berthe, who kindly took her in. Marie wasn't the only one; through my efforts and Sister Berthe's compassion, others found refuge with the sisters. Many of them later built successful lives in Montréal.

When the summer holidays ended, I returned to Miragoâne, happy to reunite with my dear friend Josie but still carrying lingering feelings for Henry. He frequently lingered outside the sisters' house or church, watching me from a distance. Although he wrote letters, I rarely responded. My reluctance stemmed from the trauma of our past encounter, which had shifted my feelings toward him.

Back in Miragoâne, Josie shared her concerns about a man pursuing her. Her advice about Tony was cautious: ―If you don't love this man, don't marry him. You'll only face unhappiness.‖ Her words echoed in my mind as Tony's persistence continued. Despite my reservations, loneliness and a sense of duty led me to say yes.

The decision to marry Tony weighed heavily on me. My close friends were gone, and the convent no longer felt like home. Though I did not love him, I felt trapped by societal expectations and the desire to escape my circumstances. Preparations for the wedding began, led by Sister Berthe and my family. Despite the generous efforts, I approached the marriage with dread rather than joy.

My brief visit to Tony's family in Cayes during the holidays cemented my unease. Their house, infested with bedbugs and facing a cemetery, was far from welcoming. Tony's behavior and expectations further alienated me. Desperate for relief, I sought refuge with his cousin, Rosita, who offered me kindness and shelter.

When I returned to Port-au-Prince, I confided in Sister Berthe about my experiences in Cayes. She advised me to cancel the wedding, but I felt trapped by the weight of public knowledge and social obligation. Preparations continued, and I resigned myself to a decision that felt inevitable but hollow.

On the day of the wedding, I left the convent with immense regret. My years with the nuns, especially under the guidance of Sister Berthe, had been a haven of learning and growth. Though my departure marked a new chapter, the lessons and strength I gained from the sisters remained with me, shaping my resilience in the face of an uncertain future.

6

Sixth life

A Sad Marriage

Newlywed in Miragoâne

I traveled to Port-au-Prince a week before my wedding, staying at Sister Berthe's to finalize the preparations. The night before the marriage, sleep eluded me as memories of my late mother and thoughts of my sister Irène in Canada filled my mind. The closer the reality of marriage came, the more it felt like a trap. What had once seemed like a harmless game now loomed as a serious, irreversible commitment. I wanted to run, but it was too late. That night, my turmoil manifested in haunting nightmares, leaving me drenched in sweat and tears when I woke.

The morning of my wedding, a heavy sadness settled in my chest. While attending to minor errands before my appointment at the hairdresser, I couldn't stop crying. Sister Berthe tried to console me, saying, —You should be happy on the morning of your marriage.‖ But I could only reply, —I cannot.‖ My tears flowed from a deep well of despair; I knew why I was crying, and so did she. I didn't love this man. As regret washed over me, one thought echoed in my mind: *How will I live with someone I do not love?*

At eleven, I arrived at the studio, my face swollen with tears. The girls there scolded me gently: —If you keep crying, your face will be a mess. Forget about the marriage—pretend you're acting in a play. Imagine yourself a star and think of something joyful.‖ Their words planted an idea that has stayed with me: when life feels unbearable, I pretend I am an actress in a role. That day, I clung to memories of happier times—of my childhood with my brother Robert, our mischievous games, and the warmth of my mother's presence. I silently prayed to Jesus and my mother for strength.

When I left the studio, the tears had stopped, but the sadness lingered. Back at the sisters' residence, it was time to dress for the ceremony. Christiane, a boarding teacher, assisted me in my sister Irène's absence. Sister Berthe came by to check on me and expressed her delight at how beautiful I looked. But inside, I felt numb. It was as though I were trapped in a surreal dream. Like an automaton, I followed the instructions given to me. When the time came, I descended to the great hall, where family and friends had gathered. The dream continued—people surrounded me, yet I saw no one, not even the bridegroom. My sole focus was to endure the day.

The church was just a short walk away, and we went there together. I recall nothing of the ceremony itself. My body was present, but my spirit drifted elsewhere, detached from the world. Reflecting on it later, I realized I wasn't truly alive in those moments. I don't even remember uttering the words, ―Yes, I do.‖

The reception was a blur. It wasn't until I arrived at the dining hall that the reality of my marriage began to sink in. The sisters had orchestrated a stunning event: a lavish cake, a beautifully set table, and an atmosphere of celebration. I was genuinely touched—it was far more than I had expected. Sister Berthe had spared no expense to make the day memorable.

When the festivities ended, I changed out of my wedding dress, and we left for the hotel. I can't recall its name, but that was where my life with Tony officially began. The weight of being alone with a man I didn't love triggered a physical reaction—I had an asthma attack. Tony tried to help, propping my head up with pillows and the little suitcase, but nothing eased my struggle to breathe. That night marked the beginning of a union defined not by love but by fear.

The Birth of Max

Tony's desire for a child was undeniable, and within two months, I was pregnant. From the first day, however, I felt unwell. Despite my constant discomfort, I had to continue working, knowing that hiring a replacement would cost money we couldn't spare. True to his habits, Tony continued to leave me alone every afternoon to play cards. His absence stretched into the evenings and weekends, leaving me to confront my solitude. For some women, perhaps this wouldn't matter, but for a young woman like me, with no close confidants, the loneliness was suffocating. Any attempt to step outside and meet a friend would have branded me a "little whore" in his eyes. Yet he felt no such constraints, doing as he pleased without regard for me. He barely spoke to me, except at night when he climbed on top of me without affection or tenderness. If I resisted, he forced me, ignoring my protests.

Pregnancy brought with it an onslaught of ailments. Nausea, though expected, persisted until the very end. Black spots dotted my skin, incessant itching plagued me, and I developed painful abscesses that deepened my misery. ―I never want to be pregnant again,‖ I told myself repeatedly. When Tony left for Cayes one time, I suffered another asthma attack. Fortunately, his cousin Jacques was there to summon the sisters, who sent someone to stay with me. My friend Laura also stepped in, administering the doctor-prescribed injections that eased my suffering. Even in Tony's absence, strange occurrences unsettled me—noises on the rooftop at night that left me sweating in fear. Upon Tony's return, I told him about these disturbances. His response was cryptic: ―You'll see; the noises will come, and I'll deal with them.‖ True to his word, he shouted into the night, and the noises never returned.

As the months passed, the time to deliver my baby drew near, but ominous warnings clouded the anticipation. Strangers stopped me in the street, urging me to tell my husband to act, lest I die giving birth. Tony dismissed these concerns outright, telling me not to listen. A week before delivery, my aunt Dieula rushed me to her home after her psychic friend had foreseen blood and death unless specific rituals were performed. Despite not having everything the psychic requested, he reassured me: —There will be much struggle and blood, but not death. Keep the faith and pray.‖

On the morning of November 2nd, the contractions began, and by the evening of November 6th, I was still in labor. The ordeal was excruciating—the baby refused to descend, choking me instead. In despair, I cried out to my deceased mother, my father, Jesus, and the Virgin Mary for deliverance. My hospital room became a revolving door of visitors, leaving me no peace. By the time my aunt Dieula arrived, I was no longer in pain but was growing weaker. She prayed over me, placed something under my head, and assured me, —All will be well. Trust me.‖ That night, I dreamt of a radiant woman dressed like the Virgin Mary, who smiled at me with a serenity that gave me hope. When I awoke, labor pains resumed with a renewed urgency.

The doctor decided on a cesarean, but later I learned it would have killed me due to my weakened state. The baby seemed determined to be born, and the nurses hurried me to the delivery room. Without anesthesia, they cut me on both sides to make room for him. The pain was unimaginable, but finally, my son was born—a healthy boy. My prayers had been answered, and I thanked God for guiding us through the ordeal.

After the delivery, I lost my voice and had to communicate through gestures. Exhausted but relieved, I named my son Berthold Max, in honor of Sister Berthe, who had become a maternal figure to me. Tony, however, reversed the names, putting Max first. For the moment, I didn't argue; I was too tired to care. A sedative eased the pain from my cuts, and I was left to rest.

The next day, Max was thriving, but I was weak and unable to speak much. My first words were resolute: ―I will never have another child.‖ Visitors filled the room, offering their support, but when the night came, I was left with my godmother Ruth, who stayed by my side as was customary in Haiti. Late in the night, a terrifying noise startled me awake—a choking sound near the baby's cradle. When I turned to look, I saw blood everywhere. Panic ensued as the nurse took the cradle away, and I was left pleading with God to spare my child. The doctors were baffled. They found no source of the blood but declared he lacked enough to survive. The only solution was to take him to Port-au-Prince immediately.

Despite my own fragile state, I insisted on going with Max. The doctor refused, warning Tony that my condition was too precarious. Ultimately, Max was taken to Port-au-Prince without me, accompanied by family and a nurse. Alone at home, I endured excruciating pain from my unhealed cuts and engorged breasts. I cried through the nights, unable to care for myself, let alone my child. My neighbors called aunt Dieula and Claire, who sought help from Aunt Lisette. Using herbal steam baths, they gradually nursed me back to health.

When Max returned, he was healthy and thriving, but I was still too weak to care for him. My friend Laura took him daily for a month while I recovered. At night, his cries terrified me, as Haitian superstition warned that they might attract evil spirits. Tony, insensitive as ever, spanked Max to silence him, leaving me sobbing and pleading for gentler treatment. Eventually, I hired a servant, Louise, to care for Max. Aunt Dieula, his godmother, also took him in for a while, keeping him beside her at night to comfort him. Under her care, he stopped crying, and I visited him twice a day, grateful for the peace he found in her home.

7

Seventh life

A Secret Love

An Unexpected Declaration

Since Max's birth, a profound sense of disgust began to consume me. Life in Haiti had become suffocating, and I found myself yearning to escape, even if it meant leaving my baby with aunt Dieula. This thought alone filled me with guilt, but the despair I felt in my marriage overshadowed everything. Tony's presence had become intolerable—his nightly card games stretched longer than ever, leaving me alone in the house with his cousin Jacques. Max was three months old, and though his absence from the house was supposed to make things easier, my boredom and restlessness only deepened. My only solace came from occasional visits to Nélia's, but these were fleeting distractions from an increasingly unbearable reality.

Tony's absence created a vacuum that Jacques unintentionally began to fill. Unlike Tony, Jacques was attentive and present, focused on his studies and sports, and uninterested in the vices that consumed my husband. Despite being younger than me, Jacques quickly became my confidant. We talked about everything, and I found myself relying on him emotionally in ways I hadn't expected. I convinced myself there was no ulterior motive, but deep down, I sensed that this growing friendship was evolving into something more. I clung to denial, not just to protect our relationship, but to avoid confronting the betrayal it represented to my marriage.

As the days passed, this forbidden feeling began to take root. A wave of anxiety accompanied it, leaving me physically and emotionally drained. I couldn't eat, and everyone assumed my misery stemmed from missing Max, who was still with aunt Dieula. The truth, however, was something I couldn't confide to anyone—not even Jacques. When he practiced karate in the downstairs room, I often watched from the doorway, but even that had become unbearable. Each accidental touch of his hand sent shivers through me, sensations I had never felt for another man. It was overwhelming, stronger than anything I had ever known, and it terrified me.

To cope, I began avoiding him. I stopped sitting with him on the balcony and avoided the basement where he practiced his sports. Yet, despite my efforts, the tension lingered, making every shared moment feel charged and unbearable. At the same time, Tony's presence in the house became increasingly ghost-like. When he did make love to me, it felt mechanical and hollow. I endured it, praying for it to end quickly, as the chasm between us widened into something insurmountable.

The Beginning of a Double Life

One day, I decided to write Jacques a letter to declare my love to him. Since he was my husband's cousin, I was treading on slippery ground. His reaction was unpredictable, and I wondered if he would show the letter to Tony. I told myself: ―I give up. I can not hide this anymore; I have to do this.‖ I have transcribed everything that I wrote to him then since it is still fresh in my memory:

My dear friend,

What I am about to confess to you is very painful for me. I am forced to gather all my courage with both hands to do this because I cannot stand it anymore. For a while now, I have suffered, and I can no longer live like this. I love you. And that is it; I love you. I know that you are Tony's cousin, but I do not want to suffer anymore. I do not know your feelings. If ever you do not love me, say nothing to Tony. You can simply answer me that you don't, and I will know what to do, because I can no longer live without you. I do not love Tony. I have never loved him. And I have never felt for someone what I feel for you.

It was the Easter vacation in Haiti. My baby was 5 months old, and Jacques had not returned with his parents. He still stayed at the house. Tony was never there, even during the day. The servant, Zita, went back home around 4 o'clock, and Max was staying at Dieula's with his babysitter. We were always alone.

In my letter, I had also warned Jacques: "If ever you don't love me, we will not be able to remain friends like we were." After getting the letter, he had changed. He had become pensive; now, he was the one who could no longer eat. I sensed that he could not live as before. He no longer practiced his sports. At least one week went by before he answered me. I found the wait excessively long. I also feared that he would show the letter to Tony. If he had done so, I truly would have given up, because I did not love Tony. I had made up my mind to give up everything. I am this way. I always take risks; if it does not work, I accept the situation and do something else.

Finally, one afternoon, Jacques and I were alone. He announced to me: "I have something for you." My heart was pounding. I did not know yet what his answer would be. He gave me a letter. I read it, and I understood that the feeling was mutual. I did not even have the time to say a word because we were already kissing each other. It happened all by itself, without useless words. We only said that we loved each other and we were already in his room. We made love, and we were happy, as if nothing else had ever existed.

Legend of the black and white photography

1. Enice in Haiti (1965)
2. Enice at her wedding
3. Enice's mother
4. Enice's father
5. Wedding cake
6. Dadia and her daughter
7. Dadia, as a young lady
8. Sister Berthe in Haiti (1969)
9. Jacques, Max and Riva at the Port-au-Prince Airport
10. Max, seven years old (1976)
11. Max, three months old

Legend of the colour photographs

1. Enice pregnant with Natatsha with Max (1972)
2. Liliane B. and Natatsha (1973)
3. Enice in New York (1970)
4. Enice in Longueuil (1971)
5. Natatsha with Max at Liliane B. (1972)
6. Max and Natatsha (1972)
7. Max and Francine (1971)
8. Max and Francine (1971)
9. Max and Natatsha, 14 months old (1973)

Page before

Miragoâne, Haiti

View of the south-west part of the city, in the years around 1980.

Photo:

Jean-Richard Raphaël

Budding Love

For the first time, I let myself go with a man in a way I never had before. With Jacques, I felt alive—happy, empowered, and transformed into someone entirely new. He, too, seemed changed, becoming more confident and assertive. Each afternoon, once the house emptied, we found solace in each other, making love in a world of our own. Tony, too consumed with his women and card games, didn't even notice the shift in me or the happiness that had blossomed within. The growing lightness in my heart was invisible to him, as was the growing distance between us.

Though my secret affair with Jacques brought me joy, the desire to leave Haiti lingered in my mind. I often discussed my plan with Jacques, who encouraged me. He could see that my life with Tony was a constant torment—a household steeped in tension and misery. That summer, I finally voiced my intentions to Tony: I wanted to leave for the United States. It wasn't a conversation so much as an announcement. He barely reacted, perhaps already anticipating my departure as a path to his freedom. Over the summer months, I traveled frequently between Miragoâne and Port-au-Prince, making arrangements for my escape. One of these trips was with Jacques, and for a fleeting moment, life felt almost perfect. Jacques and I shared a profound love that made me feel free, even in the face of so many constraints. Tony, true to form, refused to accompany me on any of these trips, leaving me to navigate everything on my own.

Meanwhile, Max remained with aunt Dieula, thriving under her care. His babysitter provided additional support, which eased my worries about leaving him. I reassured myself that he was in good hands and that my departure was not abandonment but a step toward securing a better future for both of us. I made peace with the idea of leaving Tony behind. In truth, I felt no sadness at the thought of abandoning him; he had made it clear that my absence would only serve his selfish pursuits. Fifteen years my senior, he seemed content to live off whatever money I sent back from New York. When I learned that he had quit his job soon after I left, I wasn't surprised—he openly bragged to others that he no longer needed to work because his wife had gone to America to support him.

In August, my friend Nélia left for Canada, marking another farewell that heightened my awareness of how much I was leaving behind. By September, it was my turn to leave Haiti. On the day of my departure, Jacques, Tony, and my little nephew Romy accompanied me to the airport. As I boarded the plane, I knew I was walking away from a life that had suffocated me. I chose New York because it offered possibilities that Haiti could not: political and social stability and a future for Max and me. Haiti, with its volatile politics and limited opportunities, held no promise for us. ―Seize this chance while you're still young,‖ I told myself. ―Later, it will only become more difficult.‖

Though resolved, I left with a heavy heart, burdened by uncertainty. I was young, stepping into a foreign land where I knew almost no one. The weight of this decision didn't fully sink in until I was airborne. I realized I was searching for something elusive, something undefined. I carried only the certainty that whatever I sought, I would eventually find it, but at great cost. I didn't yet know the extent of the challenges awaiting me, but I braced myself for the hardships ahead.

8

Eighth life

Hardships in The United States

First Steps in New York

The plane ride to New York filled me with hope and the illusion that my journey would be simple. My brother Alain was already in the city, but I had no way to contact him. All I had was the phone number of a cousin I had never met and the address of Érik, a friend of Tony's, where I was supposed to stay. The moment I stepped off the plane at Kennedy Airport, I was overwhelmed by the vastness of the terminal and the sheer diversity of people. My attempts to navigate this unfamiliar world were clumsy; I spoke to strangers in French or Creole, asking, ―Do you know Érik?‖ Most responded with puzzled looks or in languages I didn't understand—English, Spanish, even a dismissive "Nada."

It didn't take long to realize that this wasn't Haiti, where everyone seemed to know everyone else. Here, the faces were different, and the connections I had counted on didn't exist. A doorman noticed my confusion and kindly directed me to a taxi. With some difficulty, I managed to show the driver the address in Manhattan, and we set off. As we drove, I marveled at the bright lights, bustling streets, and constant motion of the city. It felt like daytime despite the late hour. I couldn't help but imagine my arrival at Érik's as a new beginning, one filled with possibility.

When we reached the address, the building seemed imposing and unwelcoming. Inside, the doorman rang the bell for apartment 6C, but there was no response. Though he was certain someone was inside, no one came to the door. Panic began to set in. I remembered the number my cousin Ida had given me for another relative in Brooklyn. With the doorman's help, I called her, and my aunt Julia answered. Hearing my predicament, she assured me I could stay with her and gave me directions to her house. It was already past 11 p.m., and I felt lost, exhausted, and unsure of what to do next.

Just then, a tall American man stepped out of the elevator and asked about the situation. After hearing my story, he offered to drive me to Brooklyn. The doorman vouched for him, reassuring me that everything would be fine. Still, fear gripped me. The man was as tall as a giant, and I had never encountered anyone like him before. As he loaded my luggage into his car, I silently prayed for protection. Every time he stopped at a red light, he explained why—a strange gesture that gradually eased my fears. By the time we reached my aunt's neighborhood, I felt strangely safe, as though he were an angel sent to guide me.

Brooklyn at night was eerily quiet, with deserted streets that heightened my anxiety. The man carried my heavy suitcase on his back as we walked to my aunt's building. He even ensured I stood in front of the peephole when he knocked so my aunt could recognize me. Once inside, I thanked him repeatedly, overwhelmed by his kindness. After he left, I shared my story with my aunt and briefly updated her on family matters before heading to bed. That night, I felt both older and more vulnerable, knowing this arrangement was only temporary and that I had to secure a place of my own.

The following morning, my aunt served me breakfast, and I spent hours observing the bustling activity outside her window. The street scenes were mesmerizing—vendors setting up stalls, children being taken to daycare, and groups of people gathered with coffee cups and paper bags. It was a world unlike anything I had known. Yet, despite my fascination, I couldn't forget my pressing goal: finding either Érik or my brother Alain. Repeated attempts to contact Érik that day were fruitless, leaving me anxious and tethered to the apartment, afraid to miss his call.

Two days later, Érik finally called and came to pick me up. He explained the intricacies of navigating the subway and brought me to a woman's apartment in the Bronx where I could stay temporarily. The apartment was cramped, and I was given a small sofa in the living room, divided from the rest of the space by a folding screen. I had no privacy, and my belongings remained in my suitcase due to the lack of storage. The woman, though polite, made me uneasy. Something about her demeanor suggested she couldn't be trusted. Despite my reservations, I thanked her for her hospitality and settled in, knowing I had no other option.

Érik helped me begin the process of finding work. With his guidance, I navigated the city and eventually secured a job in a belt factory. It was grueling work—standing all day, using machines to punch holes in belts—but I was grateful for the opportunity. The pay was modest, but it was a start. In the evenings, I returned to the apartment, where the strained atmosphere with my host weighed heavily on me. She was cold and controlling, restricting my use of the phone and speaking to me only when necessary. I confided my struggles to my sister Irène in Montreal, who could offer little help from afar.

A surprising turn of events brought relief. One afternoon, as I walked down Amsterdam Street, I encountered my aunt Dadia, newly arrived from Haiti. She told me she had seen Alain recently and took me to meet him. Alain, overjoyed to reconnect, insisted I leave the hostile apartment immediately and move in with him. His hotel room was modest but comfortable, and the sense of security it offered was a blessing. Together, we called Irène to share the news, and for the first time since my arrival, I felt a sense of stability. I thanked God for reuniting me with my family and giving me the strength to endure those first difficult days in New York.

Hardships in New York

My new life in New York began without delay. The day I arrived at my brother Alain's place, we wasted no time. That Sunday afternoon, he took me to the grocery store, then introduced me to some friends, Isabelle, Louky, and Metty, who lived in the same hotel. Isabelle was particularly kind, offering her support if I ever needed help. She even made us dinner, which we enjoyed before calling aunt Dadia to plan a meeting for the next day. Alain and I stayed up late that night, talking about our family and the challenges of living in New York. He generously shared advice about navigating life in the city, explaining how different it was from Haiti. He insisted I stop working at the factory in the Bronx, calling it too far and too dangerous.

The next morning, we met aunt Dadia near the subway to begin our day. Alain took it upon himself to teach us how to use the subway system, giving us tips like holding our bags securely and avoiding asking strangers for directions. After this crash course in city survival, we started our search for sewing jobs. Though neither of us had commercial sewing machine experience, Alain encouraged us to say otherwise—our basic sewing skills were enough to get us started. At the factory, they assigned aunt Dadia to a sewing machine and put me on general tasks, such as laying out fabrics and trimming threads. It was exhausting work, especially standing all day, but we managed. Alain left for his job in the afternoon, leaving me a detailed map to ensure we could find our way back.

We returned home that evening without getting lost, thanks to Alain's careful instructions. Both of us were too tired to discuss the day in detail. When we met the next morning at 6 a.m. for the commute, we exchanged brief comments about the job. Aunt Dadia admitted she was struggling to master the new machines but was determined to improve. I, on the other hand, found the standing more taxing than the work itself. Despite the challenges, we pushed through, relying on each other for support.

When I received my first paycheck, I allowed myself a small indulgence—a gold chain with an 18k earth globe pendant. It was a rare moment of pride and joy in an otherwise difficult time. Meanwhile, Alain found a lead on a better job through a young woman at another factory. She promised to speak to her boss on our behalf, and soon, we transitioned to a new workplace. The commute to this factory was even longer—an hour and a half with three train transfers and long walks. The factory, run by a French woman and her American husband, specialized in fine lingerie for Fifth Avenue. While aunt Dadia worked on sewing machines, I handled tasks like pinning nightgowns and prepping them for embroidery. The work was challenging but satisfying, and I stayed there for nearly a year. For aunt Dadia, it became her lifelong occupation; she spent 30 years at that factory.

During our daily commutes, I got to know aunt Dadia better. She was much older than me, and though I was young and physically resilient, she often struggled with the grueling routine. Running through Grand Central to catch trains was particularly hard for her. She'd plead, —Nounoune, wait for your aunt. I'm not as young as I used to be; let me catch my breath.‖ We always stuck together, especially on payday, fearing the dangers of the city.

Life with Alain was steady but emotionally draining. I missed my son, Max, terribly and thought often about Jacques, my lover, and the rest of my family. Tony, however, seemed indifferent. His letters were cold and filled with demands for money. He even claimed he would save some for me in Haiti, but I knew better. I sent money anyway, instructing him to give part to aunt Dieula for Max, pay off debts, and save the rest. Instead, he spent it all on his own pleasures, abandoning his teaching job and boasting about his wife abroad supporting him. He lied to everyone, saying I hadn't sent him a cent.

Despite my efforts to build a life in New York, I couldn't imagine staying there. I wrote to my sister Irène in Canada, asking her to send an invitation for Tony to join her there. My plan was to reunite with Tony in Canada, then return to Haiti to bring Max. Irène agreed, even purchasing Tony's plane ticket. Yet, Tony's constant demands for money made this process even harder. I struggled to meet his needs while grappling with my own challenges in New York.

Alain's struggles mirrored mine in many ways. He had spent years trying to bring his wife to the U.S., but their relationship had soured. One day, I came home to find he had torn up her letters and photos in a fit of rage, declaring he was done trying to bring her over. Though I advised him to reconsider, he seemed resolute until a perfumed letter from her arrived. That single gesture reignited his affection, and he resumed writing to her and sending money.

As for me, I continued working at Maddy's factory alongside aunt Dadia, navigating a city that was both exciting and unrelenting. My focus remained on supporting my family and finding a way forward, even as the hardships mounted.

A Secret Meeting

Life continued as usual until the day I received an unexpected call from a young man I once knew. He was the same age as me, and we had been friends in Haiti, though I hadn't seen him in years. Back then, he had pursued me tirelessly, but I wasn't interested in boys at the time—it was before I had met Henry. He was just a boy in short pants when I last saw him, and my life with the sisters took me far away from him.

When I heard his voice on the phone, I didn't recognize it. —Don't you know who this is?‖ he asked. When I admitted I didn't, he revealed his name and explained that a friend of my brother's had given him my number. He assured me there was no hidden agenda, just a desire to reconnect. Hesitant but curious, I agreed to meet him at my brother's apartment the following Friday after work.

The days leading up to our meeting felt unusually long. When Friday arrived, he showed up as promised. The moment I saw him, I was overcome by a strange sensation—a shiver that ran through me, leaving me frozen and nearly speechless. He kissed my forehead gently, a gesture that felt deeply intimate, and for a moment, neither of us spoke. When we finally broke the silence, we spoke at the same time, blurting out, —You've changed; it's been so long…‖ before bursting into laughter.

The conversation flowed naturally from there. He asked about my sister, and I asked about his life. When I cautiously inquired if he was married, he said he wasn't. I could tell he already knew I was married and had a child. His questions turned probing: Why had I married an older man? Did I love him? I answered honestly. ―I don't love him. I never have, and I never will.‖ I shared pieces of my life—my brother, aunt Dadia—but I felt uneasy, as though I was standing on the edge of something dangerous.

Then, out of nowhere, he leaned closer and asked, ―Now that we're adults, what do you think about my everlasting proposition?‖ His hand gently caressed my cheek, his smile disarming and sincere. I couldn't hold back any longer. He pulled me into his arms, and I surrendered completely.

We kissed deeply, a moment filled with an intensity I had never known. We loved each other without crossing physical boundaries, and for the first time, I understood what true love felt like. It wasn't about his looks, though he was undeniably handsome. It was his essence, his very being, that captivated me. In that moment, I forgot everything—my marriage, Jacques, even my sins. All that mattered was the connection between us.

Our relationship deepened over time. We spoke on the phone daily, and he visited me weekly. Eventually, we made love, cementing the bond we had built. I even visited his place, though we both knew our situation was complicated. Neither of us had residency visas; he would need to marry someone with legal status, and I still needed to return to Haiti to bring my son and later move to Montreal. These practicalities cast a shadow over our love, making every meeting bittersweet.

When the time came for him to marry for his residency, we shared one final, heart-wrenching moment. On the day of his wedding, just before he went to church, we made love for the last time. I told him I couldn't continue—it was too painful. Though we stayed in touch by phone, I stopped meeting him. He called repeatedly, even reaching out to aunt Dadia, who knew about our secret. But I refused. I told him I loved him, but it was best to part ways. —You need to think about your future, and I need to think about mine, I said.

Years later, our paths crossed again by chance. I was with my second husband on a trip to Haiti—the first time I had been back in over a decade. He was there too, still as attractive as ever, and still unmarried. We avoided private meetings, knowing the temptation would be too strong, but our glances and brief conversations spoke volumes. Once, in Montreal, I saw him unexpectedly in a building stairway. My heart nearly stopped. He took my hand, kissed my forehead, and said, ―I still think about you.‖ That simple gesture carried a world of meaning.

Even after leaving my first husband, I never reached out to him. I didn't want to tarnish the purity of what we had shared. Aunt Dadia often tells me that whenever he sees her, he asks about me and wants to know if I'm happy. I'm comforted to know he's doing well. Sometimes, I dream about him, especially during moments of sadness. Perhaps if we had married, our love wouldn't have endured. Perhaps. But one thing is certain: I'll carry the memory of him in my heart for the rest of my life.

Nanny in Connecticut

When I began searching for a nanny position, I was met with challenges. Without American residency, my options were limited. Finding work involved combing through newspaper classifieds and hoping for opportunities. Life at my brother Alain's place was stable at first, but one Friday night, everything changed. Alain came home in an unusual state. Typically, he stayed out late on Fridays, having a few beers with his friend Metty. However, that night, I was startled awake to find him drunk, behaving erratically. He mumbled incoherently, and his words about sex were unsettling. Fear consumed me—I worried he might lose control and hurt me.

Panicked, I hastily grabbed a few belongings, washed, dressed, and left for Aunt Dadia's house in tears. She was alarmed but listened as I explained what had happened. She reassured me despite dealing with her own troubles. We spent the night walking on Broadway, sharing our burdens, and praying at church. By the time we returned to Alain's place early the next morning, he was gone. We prepared dinner together, and when Alain returned later that evening, he appeared embarrassed but unsure of what I had shared with Aunt Dadia. We never discussed that night again, but the tension lingered.

Determined to leave Alain's home, I informed him I would start searching for work elsewhere. My departure from my factory job came with a bittersweet farewell—I had grown fond of my boss and my co-workers, especially Aunt Dadia, who would continue working there for 30 years. I promised to visit her every weekend. The following weekend, with Alain's help, I scanned the classifieds and found a promising nanny position. A woman who spoke French offered to meet me at a luxurious Fifth Avenue apartment. It felt like divine intervention. By Monday, I started my new job with a family of four in Connecticut.

The family welcomed me warmly. The lady of the house showed me their beautiful two-story home, complete with a cozy room for me, including a television. My duties were straightforward: greet the children after school, assist with morning preparations, handle light housekeeping, and wash clothes. I quickly adapted, finding joy in the children's company and the peaceful environment. On weekends, I returned to Alain's place, maintaining a balance between work and personal life.

One Friday night, however, I stayed in Connecticut for a rendezvous with my lover. It was before his marriage, and he had come to meet me. For the first time, I spent the night with him. Overwhelmed with emotion, I forgot to inform Alain of my change in plans, leading him to panic when I didn't arrive on Saturday morning. He called my employer to confirm I had gone to town, but by the time I arrived, he was visibly worried. I apologized, fabricating an excuse about missing the train. It was the first time I lied, but my happiness overshadowed any guilt.

Three weeks later, I left my nanny position. The four months I spent there allowed me to save enough money to send Tony funds for his passage to Canada. Afterward, I transitioned to a Bronx factory where plastic cosmetic bags were made. There, I learned to sew on industrial machines, picking up basic Spanish from my Hispanic colleagues. However, the factory's location was dangerous, and traveling at night was a constant source of fear. I carried a rosary for protection and avoided overtime whenever possible.

Alain's wife eventually joined him in New York, prompting me to find new lodging. After two months of staying with a woman Alain knew, I moved back in with Alain and his wife, though tensions quickly arose. Ida, his wife, despised me and often left me without food, spreading lies to Alain. It was reminiscent of my childhood in Haiti. By the time I purchased my plane ticket to Haiti, I felt utterly drained. I counted the days until I could leave New York and be reunited with my son.

On December 31, 1970, I left New York. My departure was marked by exhaustion and relief. Even Alain, who didn't help me with my bags, seemed indifferent. I vowed never to return to New York except as a tourist. Despite the hardships, the city had taught me invaluable lessons. I gained resilience, independence, and a deeper understanding of life's challenges.

New York was a paradox—intimidating yet mesmerizing. Its vast architecture and vibrant streets offered beauty and energy, but living there was a different story. I loved walking through Central Park, praying in the church on Amsterdam Street, and window shopping on Broadway. I marveled at the music of the early Seventies, from Michael Jackson's rise to the Beatles and Elvis Presley's final days. These small joys provided a reprieve from the overwhelming reality of city life.

As I reflect, I realize that New York shaped me in ways I never expected. It was a city of dreams, but for me, it became a crucible—a place where I learned resilience and independence. I am grateful for the lessons but have no desire to relive them. The city remains a place I cherish visiting, but my heart belongs to simpler, more grounded experiences.

9

Ninth Life

Passage Through Haiti

Reunion with my Son

On New Year's Eve, December 31, 1970, I arrived to find my brother Raymond, Jacques, and another friend waiting for me. My son wasn't there; he was too young to make the trip. Seeing Jacques filled me with happiness, but I had only one plan—I would not stay in Port-au-Prince. I needed to be in Miragoâne to spend midnight and New Year's Day with my child and Aunt Dieula. Raymond rented a small truck, and we set off amidst heavy traffic on rough roads. When the truck couldn't climb Morne Tapion, we had no choice but to walk for over an hour.

By the time we reached Miragoâne, it was dark, but the town was alive with the energy of New Year's Eve. My son was already asleep when I arrived. I kissed him gently, overwhelmed with joy to see him and Aunt Dieula again. He had grown so much. As I had requested, Aunt Dieula had prepared cabri—a dish made from giblets—alongside pureed pois pigeon and white rice, my favorite meal. Hunger made every bite more satisfying. After dinner, I walked to Bord-de-Mer to greet my godmother and my sister Claire, who were busy with their yearly tradition of deep-cleaning their homes for the New Year—a custom in Haiti. It felt wonderful to be surrounded by family, sharing this moment with Jacques, our secret love hidden from everyone else.

Back at Aunt Dieula's, I slept beside my son. The next morning, he woke to find me there. His initial shyness melted quickly as we embraced, his wide eyes gazing at me with love. He needed affection—a warmth I had not been able to give him before. When he was just a baby, I entrusted him to Aunt Dieula, his godmother, because of my fragile health. His cries at night terrified me, as I feared werewolves might come. His father, Tony, spanked him even as an infant, which drove me to seek help. Aunt Dieula, with the support of her nanny Lisette, took him in. But during my time in New York, he fell gravely ill. Aunt Dieula never told me; she didn't want me to worry. Now, hearing how close he had come to death filled me with gratitude for her care and sorrow for the time I had lost with him.

New Year's Day brought a steady stream of visitors to our yard. Aunt Dieula brewed her famously thick and strong coffee, served without dilution, as neighbors dropped by to sip and chat. True to form, she playfully scolded early visitors, pretending she wasn't awake, though everyone knew her routine. Watching her interact with the community was a joy, a testament to her vibrant spirit.

Each meal with my son became a ritual that both amused and moved me. Aunt Dieula prepared his bread soup each morning, a task that took nearly two hours. She fed him patiently, spoon by spoon, and used a little wooden branch as a mock threat to encourage him to swallow. At noon, the same ritual played out, with her humor and care shining through.

Though I spoke to him in French, he answered in Creole, a language I hadn't spoken much in years. It was hard to understand him at first, but we found our rhythm. I also learned the disturbing news that someone had allegedly tried to harm him during my absence—a story Aunt Dieula kept from me to avoid causing alarm. I didn't know whether to believe it, but the thought haunted me.

Tony, his father, had not contributed a cent to his care, though I had sent money faithfully every month. Instead, he squandered the funds on other women. I brought receipts of my payments to prove to anyone who doubted my efforts. The burden of his neglect fell entirely on me, yet I took solace in knowing I had done my part.

After the holidays, I traveled to Port-au-Prince to arrange my son's passport so we could return to Canada together. Once the paperwork was underway, I returned to Miragoâne. I rehired Zita, a former maid, to help with meals and laundry during my stay. Those weeks in Haiti were a mix of rest, visits with friends, and cherished moments playing with my son. I even carved out time to share quiet happiness with Jacques, who brought love and light into my life despite the complexities of our situation.

As my departure approached, I felt torn. Leaving Haiti meant security and a fresh start in Canada with my son, but it also meant saying goodbye to Jacques, Aunt Dieula, and the community that had cared for my child in my absence. At the airport, surrounded by family and friends, I hugged my son tightly, holding onto the promise of a better future together. Haiti faded into the distance as the plane took off, but its imprint on my heart remained—a mix of love, sorrow, and resilience that would carry me into the next chapter of my life.

Meeting Jacques Again in Haiti

Seeing Jacques at the airport, I felt a wave of emotion. He was waiting for me, his presence unmistakable amidst the bustling crowd. That evening, after reaching Miragoâne, we couldn't find a moment alone together. My focus was on my child—I wanted to spend at least two days entirely with him. Jacques understood and waited patiently.

On the third day, we visited the family home where only Raymond lived. As soon as we were alone, we embraced and kissed, a reunion charged with longing. Words were unnecessary; our connection was palpable, and we spent the afternoon in each other's arms. Jacques confessed how much he had missed me and thought about me, and I told him I had felt the same. Happiness enveloped us. Later, at Aunt Dieula's, we continued to steal glances, savoring the moments we shared. That night, we slept in the same bed, our love hidden from the world. If Aunt Dieula noticed, she kept her observations to herself.

When Jacques had to travel to the Cayes, I decided to join him. Before leaving, I gave Aunt Dieula some money to cover expenses during our absence. It was carnival season, and I had no interest in the Mardi-Gras celebrations. Jacques' father had a car, and we ventured far, our journey filled with laughter, love, and the carefree spirit of youth. We made love under the open sky and in the woods, feeling invincible. At night, we pretended to sleep separately—he in his bed and I in mine—only for him to tiptoe to me. Our passion was consuming, leaving little time for food or rest. I loved him deeply, and he loved me, but this love was different from what I had experienced with my New York friend.

Returning to Miragoâne, I spent a week devoted to my son. I cherished every moment, watching him sleep and grow more comfortable in my presence. Yet, at night, I reunited with Jacques, our time together filled with an intensity that only deepened our bond.

We eventually returned to Port-au-Prince for me to handle the necessary paperwork for my passport and Canadian visa. Jacques stayed close, and we never lost sight of each other. It was during this time he confessed he had been seeing two women while I was in New York—one a neighbor and the other someone he described as a passing distraction. At first, I was hurt by the revelation, but as I reflected on my own situation, I realized we both had sought solace during our separation. His honesty and reassurance mended any hurt feelings, and our love remained strong.

Then, I fell ill. For two days, I suffered from a fever that no medication could break. Aunt Dieula, in her resourceful way, prepared a potent remedy. She massaged me, gave me a bitter concoction to drink, and stayed by my side as I perspired through the night, changing my clothes three times. By morning, the fever had vanished. When I asked what she had done, she simply replied, —You're healed, and that's all you need to know.‖ Her care and love reminded me of the unbreakable bond we shared.

Not long after, my sister sent plane tickets for me and my son. Tony claimed he would arrange his papers to join us in Montreal, asking his father for financial support since he rarely worked. I had my doubts but focused on the joy of reuniting with my family in Canada.

Three months passed in Haiti—months filled with love, laughter, and memories with my son, Jacques, and Aunt Dieula. As the day of my departure arrived, Jacques, Rivard (my sister Claire's child), Raymond, and others accompanied me to the airport.

Leaving Haiti was bittersweet. I felt relief knowing I would finally build a life with my son in Canada, away from the insecurity of my homeland. But the sadness of leaving Jacques, Aunt Dieula, and others I cared for weighed heavily on me. I also dreaded the inevitable reunion with Tony. My mind raced with uncertainty about what lay ahead, yet my heart found solace in the purpose of my journey: reclaiming my son and starting a new chapter of our lives together.

As the plane lifted off, I left behind a piece of myself in Haiti but carried hope for the future—a future where my son and I could find peace and build a life on our own terms.

10

Tenth Life

From Haiti To Montreal

Saint-Denis Street with Tony

During the entire trip to Montreal, my thoughts circled around one question: how would I live with a man I did not love? I reminded myself, —*Leave it in God's hands; He will guide me.*‖

When we landed on April 19, 1971, I was greeted with surprising news from the immigration officer. While I passed through with my son, the officer informed me that François Duvalier, "Papa Doc," had died. The information seemed to ease my passage, as I entered as a tourist, claiming I was visiting my sister.

At the airport's exit, Irène, Robert, and Tony were waiting for me. They embraced Max and me warmly. Seeing my siblings again after so many years filled me with joy. The car ride to Irène's place was quiet and peaceful—so unlike the chaos of New York. I fell in love with Montreal immediately. Its calm streets and clean air captivated me, and I envisioned rebuilding my family there, even if my marriage to Tony felt like a charade. —*Finally,*‖ I thought, —*we can be together, despite everything.*‖

Irène lived on Saint-Denis Street, near Rachel, in a modest apartment with a balcony. The living room, kitchenette, and bathroom in the common hallway were all well-kept. She shared the space with Robert and Tony, and soon, my son and I would join them.

Life in Montreal seemed simpler and less expensive then. After staying with Irène for a week, she arranged for the janitor to rent us an apartment in the same building for $80 a month. It was a two-room apartment with a closed bedroom, a kitchen, a shared bathroom in the hallway, and a back balcony. The tenants on our floor included Irène, a kind elderly Quebecer named Mrs. Fara, and us. On the floor below lived our cousin Viviane, her friend Dona, and Dona's girlfriend Danie. It felt like a little community. The building came fully furnished, with electricity included, and we stayed there for a year.

Spring in Montreal was still cold, with melting snow lining the streets. Irène graciously lent us her bed, where Max slept between Tony and me. I was relieved by this arrangement—it gave me a reason to avoid intimacy with Tony. After a week, we moved into our apartment, where I could no longer avoid sharing a bed with him. Each night felt like a torment. I endured his touch and feigned emotions I didn't feel, pretending for the sake of appearances. My entire being rejected him.

We agreed not to have another child, especially after I witnessed how he treated Max. When Max refused to eat, Tony would hit him, yelling until the boy was terrified. Max clung to me constantly, refusing to leave my side even when I went to the bathroom. He feared his father deeply. Only Irène and Viviane could calm him. He adored Viviane, finding solace in her presence.

After a week, I had to find work. Viviane helped me secure a job where she worked, but I needed someone to watch Max. A woman living downstairs seemed like a good option, but Max's reaction to her was telling. On his first day with her, he cried so much that I broke down in tears myself. My heart ached as I left him, promising toys and sweets he didn't care about. I started my job operating a sewing machine for $2 an hour—slightly higher than the $1.60 many earned. It wasn't far from home, so I walked to work each day. Despite the manageable commute, I only lasted two months.

Life at home grew increasingly strained. Max despised his babysitter, and I could see why. His constant crying was proof she wasn't right for him. At night, Tony's advances continued, leaving me feeling trapped. Even when I resisted, he would take what he wanted, further deepening my resentment.

When I noticed my period was late, I grew anxious. Around the same time, I reconnected with Madame Maurice, a friend from New York. She ran a boarding house in Ste-Thérèse de Blainville and introduced me to a Quebecer who cared for children. Visiting her home, I saw how well she understood children like Max. He immediately felt at ease, playing with the other kids. When it was time to leave, he kissed me goodbye without tears. I felt relieved knowing he was happy and safe, far from his father's harshness.

After settling Max, I focused on finding better work. Factory jobs paid little—$1.60 or $2 an hour—but I was determined to earn more. I left one job at noon and walked into Paris Star on Rachel Street, where I was hired on the spot for $3 an hour. The work was grueling, with no breaks, and I quit after three days. Not discouraged, I searched the classifieds and found an ad seeking someone with sewing experience and basic English skills. I called, scheduled an interview, and met the manager. He introduced me to Miss Kenny, a Jewish woman who spoke no French. She placed a bundle of blouses in front of me, and another worker demonstrated how to sew them. I picked it up quickly, and by the end of the day, I was hired for $3.75 an hour.

Excited, I rushed home to share the news with Irène and our friends. They were amazed that I had found a job paying more than $2 an hour. I explained, —*You just have to look for it.* I worked there for a year and a half before leaving factory work for good.

Despite the struggles with Tony and the heartbreak of leaving Max each day, I held onto hope. Montreal was a city of opportunities, and I was determined to carve out a better life for my son and me, no matter the cost.

Bitou's Babysitters

While Max was boarding with Madame Léon in Ste-Thérèse, her health began to decline. A friend of hers, who had taken a liking to Max, introduced me to Madame Liliane Bélisle. Madame Bélisle was a warm, maternal woman who lived in a large duplex with her husband and four children in Ste-Thérèse de Blainville. Her youngest daughter, Francine, was the same age as Max, making the arrangement even more ideal. She embraced Max as one of her own, asking him to call her —Maman Bélisle.‖ This brought me comfort—I could see how happy he was with her family.

Whenever I visited him on holidays, Max cried when it was time to leave, refusing to come home with me. Yet, his tears reassured me; they were proof of how well he was cared for. Madame Bélisle never asked for payment, but I insisted on giving her money, which she used to buy clothes and other necessities for Max. Under her guidance, Max thrived. She taught him to speak, eat properly, and adapt to a structured routine. However, his transition between homes led to a peculiar linguistic challenge. At Aunt Dieula's, he had struggled with Creole; with his nannies in Montreal, he learned Québécois French. Reconciling these influences into standard French took time and patience, but we eventually resolved it.

Max was a beautiful baby, born weighing 10 pounds, with fine hair, yellow-toned skin, and round, expressive eyes. He cried often, which I attributed to sensing my own anxiety. When he stayed with Aunt Dieula in Haiti, he became calmer, finding solace in her care. Yet, despite the affection shown to him, a sadness lingered in his eyes, one that didn't fade until he reunited with me. He clung to me, fearing I might leave again. Slowly, his confidence grew, especially after he began living with Madame Bélisle. There, his joy returned, and he blossomed into a playful, boisterous little boy.

Madame Bélisle treated Max as her own child and spoiled him with affection. Once, during an outing, his energy nearly caused disaster. While holding both Max's and Francine's hands, she momentarily lost her grip on Max, and he darted dangerously close to a train. Another time, he mischievously put dirt into the home's gas heating system. Despite his spirited nature, she loved him deeply, and I was endlessly grateful for her care.

Max spent holidays like Easter and Christmas with us but always remained wary of his father. His fear was palpable, and it was fortunate when Jacques eventually joined us in Canada. Jacques's presence brought a balance and gentleness that Max craved.

While Max adjusted to his new life, my health began to deteriorate. I missed my period, felt weak, and couldn't eat. I quickly realized I was pregnant. Pale and exhausted, I struggled through my daily routines. Tony, as always, was indifferent. When I told him I needed to see a doctor, his response was curt: —*Go alone. The hospital is close.* ‖ His lack of concern stung but didn't surprise me.

One evening, while bathing, I noticed blood in the water and panicked. The next morning, my sister Irène took me to the hospital. The doctor confirmed I was two months pregnant and instructed strict bed rest, warning that my baby's life was at risk. I knew I couldn't stop working—not with Tony's indifference and our financial struggles. That evening, I began to feel sharp pains, and Irène called an ambulance. Before it arrived, I felt something pass—an egg-shaped mass of blood. My heart sank. At the hospital, the doctor confirmed I had lost the baby. I stayed three weeks for treatment, weakened by anemia.

The loss was complex. I wasn't overcome with grief, but neither was I indifferent. I knew the child wasn't Tony's; it was Jacques's. In my heart, I believed this loss was for the best. I didn't love Tony and couldn't imagine raising another child with him. Writing about this now brings a strange sense of release—I share this truth to free myself from its shadow.

Upon returning home, I resumed my routines and soon found another job. My resilience kept me moving forward, though life with Tony grew increasingly unbearable. He gambled, ignored his responsibilities, and showed little interest in Max. Despite his family blaming me for his lack of support, I sent money to them myself, knowing it was the right thing to do.

Summer brought moments of reprieve. I spent time at Île Sainte-Hélène with friends and occasionally with Tony. Max joined us for two weeks and enjoyed trips to La Ronde, where his laughter and curiosity lifted my spirits. He adored Viviane and even Mrs. Fara, the elderly neighbor who sometimes babysat him. These brief moments of happiness reminded me of what I was striving for: a better future for Max and myself.

As autumn arrived, so did a familiar melancholy. The falling leaves mirrored the heaviness in my heart. I had never liked autumn—it felt like life itself was retreating with the changing season. My sister Irène lifted my spirits with a birthday celebration on October 1st, gathering family and friends, including Max. While I received thoughtful gifts from everyone else, Tony, as usual, gave nothing—not even a card. His indifference was a painful reminder of the disconnect between us.

Still, I focused on my son, my work, and my dreams of independence. Montreal offered opportunities, and I was determined to make the most of them. Each step forward brought me closer to the life I envisioned—a life free from Tony's shadow and filled with hope for Max and me.

My First Christmas in Montreal

My first Christmas in Montreal in 1971 brought me a sense of joy and comfort, despite the challenges in my life. I was surrounded by my son, my sister Irène, my youngest brother Robert, and friends who cared about me. Life continued as usual, though it was clear I had to shoulder most of the responsibilities. I bought winter coats and boots for myself while Madame Bélisle ensured Max was well-dressed for the cold. Tony, as always, claimed he had no money, leaving me to cover the expenses. Irène often helped me, knowing I had limited resources.

November arrived, and I prepared for my first experience of winter in Montreal. The snowfall began early, transforming the city into a pristine white landscape. Snow blanketed the rooftops, trees, and streets—a stark contrast to New York, where snow typically arrived after the holidays. I marveled at the beauty of it all but soon learned how harsh the Canadian winter could be.

One Saturday, Viviane and I went shopping on Mont-Royal Street near Saint-Laurent. The day had started mild, with clear skies, so we left without gloves or proper winter gear. While browsing in a store, I noticed snow falling outside but paid it little mind. When we finally left, the snow had piled up, the wind howled, and the streets were nearly impassable. Our hands and feet were frozen, and the bitter cold brought tears to my eyes. The journey home, though only a short distance, took over an hour of struggling against the storm.

As Christmas approached, the city came alive with festive decorations. Stores, homes, and even workplaces were adorned with lights and ornaments, creating a joyous atmosphere. Employers organized parties and handed out bonuses, adding to the holiday cheer. Irène and I attended Midnight Mass together, followed by a celebratory dinner. I had bought a Christmas tree, which Max and I decorated at Irène's apartment since her space was larger. The family and friends exchanged gifts under the tree, and for a moment, I forgot about Tony's indifference. Though his presence often brought me sadness, I was surrounded by the warmth of my loved ones. My thoughts frequently drifted to Jacques, who remained close to my heart.

As the New Year approached, many of our friends began moving out of the city. Families reunited, financial situations improved, and larger homes became a priority. Nélia and her husband relocated with their children, and Dona's wife joined him, prompting their move as well. Even Viviane, who had secured a job at a bank, planned to leave for a house in Saint-Léonard by May. This cycle of transition was typical for immigrants—starting with small, shared spaces and eventually moving into more comfortable accommodations as stability grew. Irène's apartment had long served as a hub for new arrivals, providing a place to stay and find footing. Her generosity had helped countless people, including me.

In April, we received a letter from Jacques announcing his visit in July. I suggested to Tony that we rent a bigger apartment, but he resisted, prioritizing his desire for a car over our living situation. Frustrated but determined, I devised a plan. Sitting down with Tony one evening, I laid out a solution:

—Tony, you want a car, and I want a bigger apartment with furniture. Here's what we'll do. We'll visit the bank together and apply for a loan. First, we'll price the car and the furniture, bring the bills to the bank, and they won't refuse us.‖

He hesitated, questioning how we'd manage the repayments. I proposed splitting the costs:

—I'll pay for food, electricity, the telephone, and Max's nanny. You can cover the rent.‖

Though I was taking on the heavier financial burden, it was the only way to move forward. I reassured him that Jacques's arrival could help ease the rent costs. Reluctantly, Tony agreed. A week later, we secured the loan. Tony bought his dream car—a bright yellow Véga—while I focused on furnishing our new home.

We found a spacious, affordable apartment in Longueuil with two large bedrooms, a big kitchen, a living room, and a balcony overlooking an open field. The greenery appealed to my love of nature. The apartment felt like a fresh start, and I spent April carefully preparing for the move. I shopped for dishes, furniture, and other essentials, anticipating a better life for Max and myself.

Spring brought a sense of renewal. Jean, a family friend, moved into the same building in Longueuil with his wife and children. Our moves were synchronized for May 1st, and as the day approached, excitement grew. Though I was leaving Saint-Denis Street, where so much of my journey had begun, I felt ready for the next chapter. Irène remained in the building for a while longer before eventually moving on as well.

That Christmas, despite the hardships, marked a turning point. It reminded me of the importance of family, resilience, and the hope of building a brighter future. The snow, though cold and relentless, symbolized a fresh start—one I was determined to embrace.

Longueuil

In Montreal, the traditional moving day was once the 1st of May, but by the time we relocated, it had shifted to the 1st of July. When the day arrived, my sister Irène and I went ahead to clean the apartment and prepare for the furniture delivery. The apartment was brand new, so there wasn't much to clean. We organized the kitchen utensils, dishes, linens, and clothes, making sure everything was in place before the movers arrived. When they delivered the furniture, I felt a wave of happiness seeing the new space come together.

Afterward, we drove Irène back to her place in Montreal, and when I returned to Longueuil, I found myself in a beautiful apartment with brand-new furniture and a shiny new car in the driveway. Tony, of course, was thrilled—not because he had earned any of it, but because he enjoyed reaping the rewards of others' efforts. I couldn't help but think, —*This is all well and good, but we have to work hard to pay off these debts—there's no time for laziness.*‖

Our new life in Longueuil began. I spent the weekend settling in, unpacking and arranging the apartment. Meanwhile, Tony took the car out for a spin, showing it off to anyone and everyone. He had achieved his dream, thanks to Irène and me—Irène had lent us the money for the car's down payment, a loan Tony never intended to repay. It didn't take long for the inconvenience of living in Longueuil to reveal itself. Crossing the Jacques-Cartier Bridge during rush hour quickly became a daily ordeal. Traffic jams clogged the bridge every morning and evening, no matter how early we left. I was late to work so often that I began waking up earlier and earlier, though it didn't always help.

Despite these challenges, I wanted Max to enjoy the new apartment. I brought him over for a weekend visit, but he found the place too quiet. He was used to the lively atmosphere at Madame Bélisle's and our previous neighborhood, where family and friends were always coming and going. I missed that energy too. At home, I had little to no meaningful conversation with Tony. Most of the time, he spoke to me only to discuss money or to hurl insults. Yet at night, he still demanded intimacy, which I endured without affection. To avoid adding to our financial burdens, I convinced him that we couldn't afford another child.

Simple errands, like grocery shopping, became a source of conflict. Tony frequently refused to take me to the store, and I often had to remind him, —*If you won't take me, I won't cook.* His priorities lay elsewhere, spending most of his evenings playing cards in Montreal. Eventually, I decided I'd had enough. I went out and got my learner's permit. When I returned home, I announced, —*Since you don't want to drive me anywhere, and I need the car, you'll teach me to drive. I already have my learner's permit.*

Tony hesitated but eventually agreed, seeing the practicality in my suggestion. —*When we go to Montreal,* I added, —*I can drop you off wherever you need to go and use the car for errands.‖* It seemed like a sensible solution.

The lessons began, but they were far from pleasant. Nearly every evening, he gave me driving lessons, and nearly every evening, we ended up arguing. He yelled at me constantly, his impatience boiling over into anger. The tension made the entire experience unbearable. After a week of his shouting and our endless quarreling, I abandoned the idea altogether. It simply wasn't worth the stress.

Jacques in Montreal

One evening, while Tony and I were at my sister Irène's apartment, we received a phone call from Jacques. He announced that he would arrive on Saturday, September 15th, 1972. Tony seemed thrilled—I knew why. Jacques would help him pay the rent. For me, Jacques's arrival meant something entirely different. I thought, —*Finally, the man I love will be by my side. When Tony goes out, I won't feel so alone.‖*

On the day of Jacques's arrival, we waited at Irène's, planning to leave for the airport around 7:30 p.m., as Jacques had said his flight would land at 8 p.m. Just as we were about to head out, the doorbell rang. I opened it and froze. There was Jacques, standing at the top of the stairs with his suitcase, looking like someone who already knew his way around. It was 7 o'clock. His familiar smile struck me as if I were seeing him for the first time. He seemed more mature, more serious—a man rediscovered.

Inside, everyone asked,

—Who's at the door, Enice?

Gathering myself, I answered softly,

—It's Jacques.

Their responses echoed disbelief:

—That's impossible! Immigration didn't call us. How did he get here on his own?

As Jacques stepped inside, the room fell silent. His presence was magnetic, and all eyes were on him. He greeted everyone with a cheerful, —Hello! Jacques's confidence and composure captivated everyone present. They hadn't expected such a striking, distinguished man. Even his cousin, usually quick with introductions, was momentarily at a loss. Jacques later explained that immigration had gone smoothly, and after waiting at the airport for half an hour with no one in sight, he decided to take a taxi directly to Irène's.

That evening, Irène had prepared a special dinner for everyone. The apartment was lively with about ten people, including Robert, Dona, Viviane, Laura, Tony, Gisèle's family, and others. Gisèle had recently arrived from Haiti and was staying with Irène while looking for work. The gathering stretched late into the night, full of conversation and laughter.

During the drive to Longueuil, Jacques and I spoke about Haiti. He updated me on our relatives, especially Aunt Dieula, whose news was always important to me. Aunt Dieula was like a second mother to me, stepping in after my own mother passed away. Though not a biological sister, she and my godmother Ruth were lifelong friends of my mother, whom she affectionately called *sè-m,* or ―my sister‖ in Creole. When my mother died, Aunt Dieula took on the role of caregiver, providing us with food, clothes, and unwavering support. I still remembered the day she arrived after my mother's death. As a child, I ran to her, crying and clutching her legs, declaring, ―*Aunt Dieula, you are our mother now.*‖ Her love and dedication left an indelible mark on me, and making her my son's godmother felt like the honor she deserved.

Jacques's stories about Haiti brought me a sense of connection and nostalgia. He also seemed fascinated by Montreal, asking about the landmarks we passed—the Jacques-Cartier Bridge, the Saint Lawrence River, and Longueuil itself. He was curious why we lived so far from the city. When we arrived at the apartment, he was pleased with the space. I gave him a tour, showing him the rooms and the surroundings.

That night, as I lay in bed, I couldn't sleep knowing Jacques was in the room just beyond the bathroom, so close yet so far. My mind wandered, imagining myself in his arms. But I reminded myself, —*Take your time, Enice. He's here now. You'll have plenty of time to be with him.* ‖ Meanwhile, Tony insisted on making love, as though it were some transaction involving only my body, devoid of any connection to my heart. I thought to myself, —*After tonight, we'll see what the future holds.* ‖

11

Eleventh Life Between Two Men

Happiness, Sadness, and Love

The morning after Jacques arrived, a Sunday, I woke later than usual but still before the men to prepare breakfast. I felt nervous and kept telling myself, —*Be careful, Enice. Tony must not suspect anything. Be a good actress.* Fifteen minutes later, I was in the kitchen when I heard Jacques leave his room and head to the bathroom. My heart raced wildly—fear and happiness intertwined. When he came out, he walked straight into the kitchen, his familiar smile lighting up the room. His eyes devoured me, and for a moment, it felt like no time had passed since we'd last been together.

Jacques stepped closer and kissed me on the lips. I returned the kiss but whispered urgently, —*Be careful, he's here.* He squeezed my hand, and I felt like I might faint from the intensity of the moment. Composing myself, I changed the subject, careful to keep our interaction casual. As Jacques sipped his coffee, I explained how things worked in the household—his expected contributions to the rent, food, and telephone bills once he started working. But I could tell his thoughts were elsewhere. As he put his cup down, he brushed his hand across my face. His touch was overwhelming. I whispered, —*Not now, for God's sake.* He replied softly, —*I understand, but I can't take it anymore.* I reassured him, —*This afternoon, when he goes to play cards, we'll have time.* He nodded and left the kitchen.

When Tony finally woke, he asked if Jacques was up. I told him Jacques was in his room, and Tony insisted I call him for breakfast. The three of us sat around the table—Tony across from me and Jacques beside me. The situation felt surreal. I thought to myself, —*Enice, you're caught between two men. One is your husband, whom you don't love, and the other is your lover, whom you love and desire with all your heart. Can you navigate this without losing yourself?* I convinced myself that love would prevail. My uneasiness faded, and I managed to carry on a polite conversation with both men throughout breakfast.

Afterward, Jacques helped me with the dishes, something Tony would never do. Tony went to get dressed, then casually announced that he had plans to visit friends in Montreal and wouldn't be back until 2 p.m. Relief washed over me as I realized Jacques and I would finally have time alone.

I hurried to take a shower, and when I came out, Jacques was waiting for me. He led me to his room, where we kissed passionately and let ourselves go completely. The love we shared was electric, pure, and uninhibited. For hours, we talked, laughed, and made love, unconcerned about whether Tony might return early. Jacques listened as I opened up about my struggles living with Tony and confessed that the child I had lost had been his, not Tony's. I told him I could never imagine having another child with Tony but dreamed of having one with him someday.

Eventually, I reminded Jacques, —*We need to stop now. I have to prepare dinner.* He smiled and said, —*I'll rest for a bit, then come help you.* I tidied up and began cooking, feeling a newfound energy. For the first time in a long while, I felt genuinely happy and unburdened by guilt. Love filled the air, and I couldn't hide it, though Tony seemed oblivious when he returned later. He ate dinner, took a nap, and noticed nothing amiss.

That evening, I took Jacques into the city to show him around Montreal. Though he would have preferred staying home with me, I reminded him, —*We must be careful. We'll have more time soon.* The next morning, Monday, we left the house early. Tony and I dropped Jacques off at Irène's so he could explore job opportunities with my brother Robert. After a week of fruitless searching, Tony brought Jacques to his own workplace, where Jacques was eventually hired. It worked well; Jacques could now commute with us.

Our love deepened with each passing day. Whenever Tony left, Jacques and I would steal precious moments together, making love in every corner of the house, as if the world outside didn't exist. Yet my relationship with Tony deteriorated further. Arguments became frequent, and his hostility grew. Once, in a fit of anger, Tony threatened me, —*If you ever leave me, I'll kill you. And if you try to take the furniture, I'll ruin it first.* Exhausted by his behavior, I replied coldly, —*I don't need your furniture.*

Tony's disregard for our household was infuriating. He contributed nothing financially, and I relied on Jacques's support to make ends meet. Tony's nightly advances were unbearable, and I dreaded the intimacy he demanded. It was nothing like the love I shared with Jacques, which felt natural and joyous. Jacques understood the toll this situation took on me. He began teaching me how to drive, further lightening my burdens.

Complications arose when my cousin Gisèle, who lived with Irène, began visiting us on weekends. She had developed an interest in Jacques and frequently stayed at our apartment, even sharing his room. Though Jacques assured me she wasn't his type and nothing happened, her constant pursuit irritated both of us. I had no choice but to allow her visits to avoid suspicion. Tony, oblivious to the tension, welcomed Gisèle's presence as it allowed him to spend even more time away from home.

Despite these challenges, Jacques and I remained in our private paradise. We dreamed of having a child together, imagining one with Jacques's smile, nose, and eyes. Though we knew it wasn't the right time, the desire was mutual. Our love grew stronger every day, filling my life with happiness I hadn't known in years. Despite the circumstances, we found joy and hope in each other, believing that our love could overcome anything.

The Fruit of Love

Everything seemed to be going well until the first week of October, when I began experiencing persistent nausea and stomach pains. At first, I dismissed the idea of being pregnant since I had just had my period a few days prior. Concerned, I went to Notre-Dame Hospital, where the doctors ran multiple tests over two days but couldn't identify the issue. As a precaution, the doctor suggested a pregnancy test.

After the tests, I returned home to Longueuil. A couple of hours later, the phone rang. It was a nurse calling with my results. Her voice was cheerful as she said, —*Madame, good news!* My heart skipped a beat as I asked, —*What is it?* She continued, —*You're pregnant. The doctor has referred you to Dr. Amyot in gynecology. Your appointment is in two weeks.*

The words hit me like a wave of joy. I was so overwhelmed that I barely registered the details and had to call the nurse back to confirm the date and time of the appointment. Alone in the house, I let the news sink in. My thoughts immediately turned to Jacques. I knew he would be thrilled, but I also knew the complications this pregnancy would bring with Tony.

That evening, I prepared dinner as usual, keeping my secret to myself. After dinner, when Tony went to nap, I asked Jacques to take me for a driving lesson. He understood immediately that I needed to speak with him privately. As we got into the car, I turned to him and said:

—*I don't think I'll be driving today. I have good news—and bad news.*

He smiled and asked, —*What's the good news?*

I replied softly, —*I'm pregnant.*

Jacques's face lit up with joy. He squeezed my hand, unable to kiss me in public.

—*What will we do?* he asked.

I explained, —*I haven't told Tony yet. I wanted to talk to you first and get your advice.*

Before he could respond, I added, —*Tony always ejaculates outside of me, but sometimes he immediately starts again. It's possible that some sperm could still linger.* Jacques considered this and nodded. He cautioned, —*We need to be careful. I don't trust Tony.*

Jacques admitted, —*If I had been working longer, we could have moved in together.*

I reassured him, —*I have debts with Tony. I need to settle them first. For now, we'll manage.*

The next day, I told Tony about the pregnancy after work. He seemed surprised and skeptical, saying, —*But you just had your period.*

—*The doctor says it happens sometimes,* I replied casually.

He wasn't particularly excited but asked, —*Do you think we can handle two kids?*

—*Of course,* I told him. —*We're both working, and Jacques is helping us financially.*

Tony didn't ask any further questions, but I could sense his indifference. For me, it didn't matter—this child wasn't his, and I knew it.

The pregnancy brought constant nausea, vomiting, and a lack of appetite, but Jacques's love and attentiveness kept me grounded.

We continued to share our secret moments, and his support gave me strength. I avoided Tony as much as possible, especially as his verbal abuse and financial demands escalated.

Tony often refused to pay his share of expenses, including the loan he owed my sister for the car's down payment. His indifference to our household finances frustrated me, but Jacques stepped in to help, easing the burden. Tony's control extended even to a joint savings account. While he could withdraw money freely, any attempt I made to do so resulted in a fight.

The strain of commuting from Longueuil to Montreal, coupled with my growing pregnancy, pushed me to find a new apartment. Viviane found an affordable basement apartment in Saint-Léonard, near her own. Though the rooms were small, it was manageable, and Tony's reluctance to pay more left me with no other choice. We planned to move in May.

By April, I had reached my sixth month of pregnancy. My belly had grown so large that continuing to work became a challenge. Balancing my job, the impending move, and my pregnancy was overwhelming. At my doctor's recommendation, I requested a leave of absence. My coworkers surprised me with a small celebration and a gift for the baby. Their kindness brought me a rare moment of joy.

Meanwhile, Jacques was counting the days until the baby's arrival. He frequently asked, —*What will we do after the baby is born?* I always replied with the same reassurance: —*I'm leaving everything in God's hands.*

Sometimes, he worried aloud, —*What if the baby looks like me?* I smiled and said, —*Don't worry. This baby is a child of love and will be perfect, just like us.* I often placed his hand on my belly to calm him, reminding him that our child was a blessing.

Tony remained indifferent, going about his days as though the pregnancy was of little consequence to him. I questioned my feelings, wondering if I was a monster for carrying Jacques's child while pretending with Tony. But deep down, I knew my love for Jacques was real, and this child was the fruit of that love.

As May approached, I packed up my life in Longueuil, eager for a fresh start in Saint-Léonard. Despite the difficulties, I felt hopeful for the future. The love I shared with Jacques gave me the courage to keep going, and I believed that this baby—a symbol of our love—would bring us closer to the happiness we both deserved.

Another Move

With everything packed and ready—boxes and furniture alike—we enlisted the help of friends, my sister, and Viviane for the move. We rented a truck, making it possible to transport everything in just one trip.

Jacques, as always, was a tremendous help, while my sister and Viviane assisted in setting up the new apartment. The space was much smaller than the one in Longueuil, which meant we had to be creative in arranging our belongings. Jacques's new bedroom was noticeably smaller, while the room Tony and I shared was slightly larger, allowing enough space for a cradle.

The apartment itself was modest, consisting of a narrow corridor, a small living room, and a kitchen. The washer and dryer were conveniently located in the bathroom. However, being a basement unit in a duplex, it lacked a balcony. Despite its size, it was comfortable enough for our needs.

Initially, the landlords were kind and accommodating, even allowing us to park our car in their driveway. However, their attitude shifted dramatically when we gave them notice of our intent to move at the end of our lease. Their anger escalated to the point where they forbade us from parking in the driveway and even called the police on us. The once-cordial relationship soured entirely, and they stopped speaking to us altogether.

Adding to the tension, we discovered that we were unknowingly paying their electricity bill since both units shared the same meter. Once we realized this, we decided to turn off their hot water in retaliation. The situation quickly became unbearable. While the rent was affordable, the exorbitant electricity costs made the arrangement far less economical.

Now that I had stopped working, I had more time to focus on myself, the apartment, and my son, Max. I called Madame Bélisle to let her know that I would be taking Max home at the end of the month to stay with us until my delivery. She agreed without hesitation, understanding my need to have him close during this time.

Meanwhile, my relationship with Jacques remained as strong as ever. His presence at home became more constant after an accident at work left him unable to go back for a while. Our passion for each other burned just as brightly, but it had softened into something even more intimate and tender. I felt like a truly loved and cherished woman, finding happiness and fulfillment despite the challenges of my circumstances.

Jacques contributed in every way he could, even giving me money to prepare the baby's trousseau. My sister also chipped in, helping me buy a cradle and other essentials for the baby's arrival. However, I began to notice that Jacques was growing increasingly jealous of Tony. While I rarely had to be physically intimate with Tony, Jacques understood that if it happened, it was never by choice.

When Max came home, my joy was complete. He quickly bonded with Jacques, forming a far better relationship with him than he had with his father. Max respected and listened to Jacques in a way he never did with Tony. However, Max's language issues persisted, and we often had to correct his pronunciation.

Despite his lively and boisterous nature, Max flourished under Jacques's guidance. Without Jacques's presence, I knew Tony would have resorted to his usual harshness, likely punishing Max daily. Fortunately, Tony was rarely home, which made life much more peaceful for all of us.

Though our circumstances weren't perfect, I found comfort in the small joys of my family—my son's laughter, Jacques's love, and the growing anticipation of the new life I carried within me.

A Difficult Pregnancy

As my pregnancy progressed, my belly grew so large that walking unassisted became nearly impossible. Someone always had to accompany me, especially after a frightening incident in Longueuil before our move. While walking alone to church, I tripped and fell on my stomach. The experience left me shaken, and I had to be taken to the hospital. Thankfully, the baby was unharmed, but the scare stayed with me. By the time we moved to Saint-Léonard, my belly had grown even larger, making mobility even more challenging.

One afternoon, Jacques and I went out together, running errands on Saint-Laurent Boulevard with plans to stop by my sister's on Duluth Street. As we neared our destination, I suddenly found myself unable to walk any farther. Spotting a small restaurant nearby, I insisted we go inside to rest, even though it looked far from clean.

Jacques hesitated, clearly uncomfortable, but I was adamant. *—I'm ordering a pizza,*‖ I told him, trying to justify our stop. He raised an eyebrow and asked, *—Are you sure?*‖ I nodded firmly.

When the pizza arrived, I dove in, eating voraciously. It wasn't until I was almost finished that I realized I hadn't offered Jacques a piece. Embarrassed, I held out the last portion and said, *—Would* *you like some?* He smiled gently and replied, —*No, you can finish it.* Relieved, I finished the meal, grateful for his understanding.

Afterward, I found myself unable to stand up from my chair. We sat there for another half hour, giving me time to recover. Finally, with great effort, I managed to leave, leaning heavily on Jacques as we slowly made our way to my sister's.

As I entered the final month of my pregnancy, I had a routine appointment with my doctor. After examining me, he ordered a sonogram and blood tests to check on the baby's progress. A few days later, the results brought troubling news: the baby wasn't growing as expected.

The doctor explained that I wasn't eating enough nutritious foods, like vegetables, and wasn't taking vitamins. —*You must start taking three vitamins daily,* he stressed. —*This is crucial. Otherwise, you risk losing the baby.*

Hearing this, I was overwhelmed with worry. Once I returned home, I told Jacques everything. He immediately stepped in, saying firmly, —*From now on, I'll prepare all your meals. You need to eat well for the baby.* True to his word, Jacques took meticulous care of me, ensuring I followed the doctor's advice. His efforts paid off, and the baby's condition began to improve.

Despite the challenges, there were moments of levity that brought me comfort. My son Max, now home with me, adjusted well to the new environment. On days when I needed to see the doctor or run errands, I would leave him with Viala, Dora's wife, who also had a young baby.

Viala's baby was a beautiful child, with curly black hair, round eyes, and a chubby face. Max loved spending time with them, though his comments often made us laugh. Having lived with Madame Bélisle, a Quebecer who encouraged sunbathing, Max thought it was normal to tan. He once announced to Viala, ―*I want to go out in the sun to get a tan.*‖

Amused, she laughed and replied, ―*You're already tanned! Do you want to get yourself burnt?*‖ Her teasing made everyone smile, and I cherished these lighthearted moments amidst the worries of pregnancy.

Despite the difficulties, I found strength in the love and support of those around me. Jacques's care, Max's cheerful presence, and the kindness of friends like Viala reminded me that even in challenging times, love and laughter could provide solace.

The Birth of My Daughter

I was in the final week of my pregnancy, and though I could feel the delivery approaching, there were still tasks to complete. Alone at home, I decided to visit the bank a short walk from the house. I wanted to ensure my accounts were in order before heading to the hospital. Moving around was a challenge, and the size of my belly drew stares from passersby. Two hours after returning home, the cramps began.

Jacques, who had gone to work earlier, came home to find me unusually busy. I had cleaned the entire house, packed my hospital bag, and organized everything. Concerned, he asked, —*What's going on?*

I replied, —*I'm starting to feel sharp pains in my belly and back.*

Jacques froze, unable to respond, his worry evident in his silence. He always reacted this way in moments of stress, and I could see how deeply concerned he was.

When Tony arrived, I informed him, —*It might happen tonight.*

Instead of showing empathy, he coldly replied, —*I hope it doesn't happen during the night—I need my sleep.*

His lack of affection was nothing new, but it no longer bothered me. Perhaps his indifference made it easier for me to focus on

Jacques, the true father of my child. While Tony ate his dinner without a care, Jacques barely touched his food, his sadness palpable. My son, Max, wasn't home, as I had sent him to stay with Madame Bélisle in anticipation of the delivery.

As the night progressed, the pain intensified. I couldn't sleep and found myself sitting upright with pillows propped behind me, struggling to manage the contractions. Around 10 PM, I called my sister, who advised me to head to the hospital immediately. The contractions were now coming every 15 minutes.

I woke Tony and asked him to drive me. Reluctantly, he agreed, but two hours after arriving at the hospital, the staff sent me back home, stating it wasn't time yet. Annoyed, Tony scolded me for disrupting his sleep, saying, —*Why did you bother me for nothing?*‖

An hour later, the pain became unbearable. I told him I would call a taxi if he refused to take me back. Begrudgingly, he relented and drove me to the hospital again. Before leaving, I called my sister to let her know what was happening, and she assured me she'd meet me there.

This time, the hospital staff admitted me. Tony left as soon as we arrived, unwilling to stay, but my sister remained by my side. The contractions continued through the night, relentless and excruciating. By morning, I had only dilated two centimeters, and the doctors noted that my water still hadn't broken.

I explained to one doctor that during my first delivery in Haiti, my water hadn't broken naturally, and the doctors had to intervene. Despite this information, they seemed hesitant to act. By 1 PM, the pain was unbearable, and three doctors finally came to check on me. My sister reminded them of what I'd said earlier, and they finally broke my water.

Minutes later, the baby was ready to arrive. Nurses rushed me into the delivery room, where a Haitian doctor stepped in to assist, as my primary doctor, Dr. Amyot, was attending to another patient.

As soon as I was on the delivery table, the doctor encouraged me, ―*The baby is coming—push!*‖

I summoned all my strength and, after one final push, my daughter was born. ―*Madame, it's a girl,*‖ the doctor announced.

In that moment, all my pain vanished. Overwhelmed with happiness, I whispered, ―*Thank you, Jesus,*‖ as tears filled my eyes. The nurses took the baby away to clean her, and I waited eagerly to hold her.

When they brought her back, I was stunned. She was a miniature Jacques. Her resemblance to him was undeniable, and panic crept in as I thought, ―*Dear God, please make her face change so no one notices.* Yet, I couldn't help but feel immense love for her. Holding her in my arms, I sent a prayer to God: —*Thank you for this child of love. Please guide her and protect her.*

Later, when Jacques arrived, he anxiously asked about the baby. I told him over the phone earlier that she resembled him. When he saw her, he was astonished. —*She doesn't look like me,* he said, visibly relieved.

Smiling, I replied, —*I told you to trust in God.*

Tony eventually showed up at the hospital, happy but indifferent. He visited briefly before leaving again. Meanwhile, my sister stayed by my side, helping with the baby and providing emotional support. I stayed in the hospital for five days, recovering from the delivery and my exhaustion.

Madame Bélisle visited during my stay and offered to help care for the baby, just as she had with Max. I was relieved, knowing I could rely on her once Max started school in September.

When it was time to leave the hospital, Tony and my sister came to pick me up. We stopped to collect the baby's cradle on the way home, and my sister helped set it up before preparing dinner. Viviane joined us, bringing her young daughter Micha, to lend a hand. That evening, I lay in bed, overwhelmed by exhaustion but grateful for the support around me.

As I settled into life with my newborn, the challenges of living with Tony became even more apparent. He was of little help with the baby, leaving me to handle night feedings and care on my own. His indifference pushed me further into Jacques's arms, as he continued to support me emotionally and physically.

Max returned home a week later, but he struggled to adjust. Disappointed that the baby wasn't a boy, he declared, —*This isn't my baby—I wanted one like Yvi!*‖

I patiently explained why his sister didn't look like Yvi, emphasizing that all families are different. Though he seemed to understand, his frustration manifested in bedwetting, which the doctor assured me was temporary.

With the help of Jacques, my sister, and friends like Viviane and Laura, I managed to care for my children despite my ongoing fatigue and anemia. Tony, however, remained absent and unhelpful, spending his time out with friends.

Jacques, noticing my growing unhappiness, urged me to leave Tony. —*This isn't good for you,*‖ he said. —*You'll make yourself sick.*‖

Though I wasn't ready to leave, I knew he was right. Life with Tony was becoming increasingly intolerable, and Jacques's presence was my only solace. Despite the challenges, I found strength in my love for my children and my faith in God.

Natatsha's Baptism

On the eve of Natatsha's baptism, everything seemed to fall apart. She spent the entire night crying, an unusual occurrence that immediately worried me. I called my sister, who advised me to check her temperature. When I did, it was 100.4°F. Alarmed, my sister urged me to take her to the hospital without delay. I was alone with Jacques, so he stayed home with Max while I took a cab to the hospital.

Upon arrival, her temperature continued to rise, and the doctor informed me, —*We need to admit her for monitoring and run some tests.* He added, —*She'll need to stay naked to manage the fever.*

The sight of her tiny body lying in a cradle in the intensive care unit, with an IV drip in her head and her hair partially shaved, broke my heart. The doctor suggested, —*If the baptism is important, ask the priest to perform it here in the hospital. She's very sick.*

I called Jacques to update him and asked him to inform Tony. I also reached out to my sister, who came to the hospital immediately to support me. Through tears, I confessed my fear of losing my child. My sister comforted me, saying, —*Pray to God and entrust her to Him.*

Though I tried, I was so overwhelmed and exhausted that my prayer was brief: —*Jesus, Thy will be done. You gave her to me. Please guide us and do what is best for her. Give me the strength to endure this.*

Tony arrived late in the afternoon, showing little concern. When I suggested canceling the baptism to spare our guests the confusion and to focus on the baby, he flatly refused, saying, —*The baptism will still take place.*

I was left to manage everything. I called Laura for help, as I knew I couldn't handle the preparations alone. Laura, along with my sister Irène and Viviane, arrived early the next day to prepare food for the reception. Jacques, visibly upset by the situation, told me, —*You should drop everything.* He hated crowds and was frustrated by Tony's insistence on continuing the event despite our daughter's condition.

By Saturday morning, I was exhausted and declared, —*Everyone will have to manage without me.* I left for the hospital to arrange the baptism with the priest. My daughter remained in intensive care, frail and feverish. The doctors explained she was born anemic and needed treatment to stabilize her condition. They assured me she would recover with time but advised that she stay in the hospital.

The baptism was scheduled for 3 PM at the hospital, followed by a reception at 8 PM at home. Laura's support was a godsend, as she handled the logistics while I focused on my daughter. My sister, who was the godmother, accompanied us to the hospital alongside Tony and his brother.

The priest performed the baptism in a small hospital room, a stark contrast to the joyous celebration I had envisioned. Seeing my daughter in such a fragile state was heartbreaking. Her tiny body, still connected to medical equipment, looked so vulnerable. Even in the photos, her presence is barely noticeable—only the headboard of her cradle, the godparents, and the priest are visible.

It felt as though she resented the crowd, as if she had orchestrated the timing of her illness. Jacques, too, was uneasy. He stayed on the sidelines, visibly uncomfortable with the entire ordeal. Tony, meanwhile, played the role of the proud father, though he contributed little to the preparations or her care.

As the evening wore on, I managed to host the reception despite my exhaustion. Guests from New York filled the house, and I prayed for strength to get through the night. My only consolation was that by Sunday, the visitors would leave, allowing me to focus entirely on my daughter's recovery.

For the next month, my daughter remained in the hospital, and I visited her daily. Each visit required me to wear a sterile gown, but I cherished those moments when I could hold her and talk to her. I felt her trust and warmth, and her tiny smiles reassured me that she would be okay. I prayed constantly, thanking God for giving me the strength to care for her through this challenging time.

At home, Jacques was a tremendous help. He took on much of the responsibility for Natatsha's care once she was discharged. He fed her, changed her diapers, and ensured she felt loved. She recognized him as her father and responded to him with delight.

Tony, however, was indifferent. He refused to help with either child, spending most of his time out of the house. His only contribution was organizing the baptism, and even that was done with little regard for the family's needs.

When Max returned home, he struggled with the changes. Disappointed that the new baby wasn't the boy he had hoped for, he initially rejected her, exclaiming, —*This isn't my baby—I wanted a baby like Yvi!*‖

I patiently explained that babies come in all shapes and colors, depending on their parents. Over time, he began to accept his little sister, though the transition was difficult. His bedwetting, a reaction to the new dynamics, resolved after a month.

Meanwhile, I decided not to return to factory work. With unemployment benefits, I enrolled in an English course funded by the government. This change required finding childcare for both children. Madame Bélisle graciously offered to care for Natatsha, providing a calm and nurturing environment for her recovery. Max stayed with her sister, who had a spacious home and ample time to care for him.

Despite her early health challenges, Natatsha grew into a cheerful, independent baby. She rarely cried and enjoyed her swing, laughing whenever Monsieur Bélisle sang her favorite tune, —*Natatsha cha-cha-cha-cha.* By nine months, she insisted on feeding herself, a sign of her strong-willed nature.

Through it all, Jacques remained a pillar of support. His love for Natatsha was evident in the care he provided, and his presence gave me the strength to persevere. Though life with Tony remained tense, I focused on my children and found solace in the bond I shared with Jacques.

This chapter of my life, though fraught with challenges, reinforced my faith and resilience as a mother.

Back to My Business

Enrolling in an English course brought a welcome change to my routine. Over three months, I immersed myself in learning, which lifted my spirits and gave me a sense of progress. Meanwhile, I was accepted into a nursing program at Montmorency College, scheduled to start in September. Knowing I needed an income in the interim, I found a job near our apartment in Saint-Léonard.

Jacques supported me throughout this period. He had recently bought a little Volkswagen and used it to drive me to work each morning and pick me up during my lunch break. Our midday moments became precious, as evenings were consumed by his job and the demands of our lives. His jealousy of Tony persisted, but we continued to navigate our relationship with care.

After my daughter's illness, I decided it was time to get my driver's license. Once I did, I began driving both Tony's car—which I helped pay for—and Jacques' Volkswagen to run errands. Having this newfound independence felt liberating, especially in managing my responsibilities.

Around this time, Viviane, my cousin and a close family friend, had returned from Haiti, where she had entrusted her daughter Micha to her sister Fabienne. Viviane often visited us, bringing her warmth and companionship. One holiday, while Max was staying with me, I noticed he frequently visited her apartment, which made me uneasy given the tensions that had been brewing.

One evening, Viviane came over as usual, and the conversation drifted to a sensitive issue involving my sister. As I brought it up, I saw Viviane's mood change instantly. She grew visibly upset, refusing to engage in the discussion. Despite my attempts to explain, she left abruptly, slamming the door behind her.

Max, confused and upset, ran after her, calling, ―*Viviane, come back!*‖ She didn't return. When Max visited her later, she refused to open the door. Heartbroken, he cried, ―*Mamie, Viviane won't let me in.*‖ I comforted him, saying, ―*She's upset right now. Give her time. Everything will be fine.*‖

It took years for Viviane and me to reconcile, but eventually, our bond healed, and things returned to normal.

In the aftermath of the quarrel with Viviane, I noticed a shift in Jacques. He became more insistent that I leave Tony, expressing frustration with the situation. I kept telling him, ―*It's not the right time,*‖ but his restlessness grew.

One day, I discovered the source of his unease—he had been seeing Viviane for two months. Furious, I confronted him. His explanation cut deep: ―*I can't stand watching you with Tony. You keep saying we need to wait, but I need more than this.*‖

I lashed out in anger, tearing up his new shirts and warning him to end the relationship immediately. —*Viviane thinks this is serious. You're playing with fire. Leave her alone!* After a tense discussion, he promised to stop seeing her, and for a time, peace returned.

As the apartment grew increasingly cramped, and with Tony's daughter Célia soon arriving from Haiti, it became clear we needed more space. I had already initiated adoption proceedings for Célia and started planning for her sister Edith to join us later. For their sake, I couldn't leave Tony just yet.

While searching for a larger apartment, I came across a listing in Ville d'Anjou at Place Malicorne. The building offered affordable, heated 5½ units with three bedrooms, a living room, dining room, and access to a Laundromat in the basement. The location was ideal, and Jacques accompanied me to sign the lease. Tony's approval was the last hurdle.

Initially hesitant, Tony was swayed when I pointed out the financial benefits—his sister's arrival would help reduce costs, and Jacques had agreed to contribute half the rent. I also made it clear that I would continue covering Natatsha's babysitter expenses, ensuring that Tony had no grounds for complaint.

By February, we had given notice to our landlord, who reacted poorly, even involving the police over parking disputes. Meanwhile, Jacques began to test my patience. His jealousy manifested in affairs with other women, including a Native American woman and later a Haitian girl. His justification was always the same: ―*As long as you're with Tony, I have the right to do what I want.*‖

I was consumed by jealousy and frustration. One day, I drove to the Haitian girl's house and waited for Jacques to see me outside. He understood immediately that I was serious and ended the affair. Despite the pressure from all sides, we clung to each other, though the strain of our situation was overwhelming.

Tony, oblivious to the chaos, focused only on his own desires. He insisted on sex almost every morning, ignoring my protests and excuses. I felt trapped between two men—one I loved deeply and the other who made me feel violated.

Finally, in April, we moved into the Place Malicorne apartment. It was a fresh start in a spacious and peaceful environment near the Galeries d'Anjou and Beaubien Street. The greenery and convenience of the location lifted my spirits. However, the move was bittersweet.

Though I was happy to leave the cramped Saint-Léonard apartment, I was worn down by the endless cycle of work, parenting, and managing Tony's demands. Jacques, now more settled, had stopped seeing other women. Our stolen moments during the day became a source of comfort, though the nights with Tony remained unbearable.

Starting in August, I would begin my nursing course, a significant step toward reclaiming my independence. Meanwhile, I worked temporary jobs to save for the move and new household essentials. It was my third move since arriving in Canada in 1971, and though I was tired of uprooting, I hoped this one would bring some semblance of stability.

12

Twelfth Life

Towards Liberation

In Ville d'Anjou

When we moved into the new apartment in Ville d'Anjou, I finally felt a sense of relief. The apartment was spacious, on the second floor, and brand new—there was no cleaning to be done. My sister Irène came to help me settle in, as always, and my friend Nélia and her family also moved into the same complex at Place Malicorne. Having a close friend nearby was comforting, especially since she had four older children who could sometimes help.

We managed to set up everything in a single day. The neighborhood was serene, with plenty of greenery, and an elementary school was right across the street. The apartment had large, bright windows that let in natural light, which I loved. It felt peaceful—a stark contrast to my previous cramped and tense living situation.

My sister Irène bought a bed for Max, my brother Robert contributed money for curtains, and Jacques purchased a dresser for the children's clothes and a bookshelf for the living room. Irène also gifted me dishes, tablecloths, and other kitchen essentials, while I bought small decorative items to make the apartment feel more like home.

When I brought Max to see the apartment, he was thrilled and kept saying how big it was. Jacques was also satisfied with our new home since he worked nearby and could come home during his breaks when he worked evenings. I cherished these little improvements, as they gave me hope that things might finally stabilize.

Tony also worked nearby, but his demeanor remained the same—perpetually unhappy and demanding. He constantly complained about money, asking Jacques for loans he never repaid. Even though we had savings, I was the one responsible for managing the household finances and paying bills. If Tony didn't contribute one week, he'd brush me off angrily: —*Don't talk to me about it.*

Jacques, seeing how much I struggled, often stepped in. He lent or gave me money to deposit into the joint account, quietly repeating: —*We can't go on like this. Once his daughter arrives, we need to move again.* I agreed wholeheartedly.

Tony treated me like a servant. I had to buy clothes for him and deal with his constant complaints about money. He joined a networking company, claiming it would bring in income, but I never saw a cent of it. His little Véga car began breaking down, and instead of addressing it himself, he relied on Jacques to assess the issues.

Even in freezing temperatures, Jacques and his friend Jean worked on the car while Tony stayed warm indoors. Eventually, the car had to go to a dealership for repairs, costing almost $800 for the brakes alone. Tony was furious about dipping into his savings, and within a month, the car had more issues. Rather than fixing it, he bought a bigger, more expensive vehicle with larger payments—an irresponsible decision that meant I had to cover even more expenses.

When I needed the car, Tony always found an excuse: —*Take Jacques' car,* he'd say dismissively. I couldn't help but suspect he had a mistress, but I didn't care. If anything, the thought of his attention being elsewhere brought me relief.

April 19th was Jacques' birthday, and I wanted to show my appreciation for all he had done for me. I decided to throw him a small party. On Friday evening, I baked a cake and prepared pâtés. Jacques came home during lunch, spotted the freshly iced cake, and declared: —*It's my birthday tomorrow, but I'm eating my cake today!* Before I could stop him, he devoured the entire cake.

A friend who was helping me laughed at his boldness, and Jacques grinned, saying, —*You can make another one for the guests.* Despite his antics, I couldn't help but adore him. He was my anchor amid the chaos.

Life with Jacques was a source of happiness, while life with Tony was a constant battle. Tony's temper and financial irresponsibility drained me. We argued about money endlessly, and his presence brought me to tears more often than not.

Jacques, on the other hand, gave me hope. Though his jealousy flared at times, he remained my greatest support. I longed for the day when this tangled situation would finally end. Until then, I found solace in the moments I shared with Jacques, cherishing the love and understanding that sustained me through the turmoil.

Some New Changes

We received a call from Tony instructing us to send a plane ticket for his daughter, who was supposed to arrive before September. I made the reservation for mid-August since she needed to start school that month, and my courses were also beginning. My schedule was chaotic—between attending classes, working shifts, cooking, cleaning, and dealing with Tony's relentless demands, I was overwhelmed. Jacques, as always, helped as much as he could, but with his own job, he couldn't handle everything.

When I suggested reducing my work hours to part-time to alleviate some of the burden, Tony flatly refused. —*If you work part-time, you can figure out how to pay your debts,* he said. His lack of empathy made everything harder.

Tony's behavior worsened. He would repeatedly assert, —*You're my wife. I have the right to make love to you every day, whenever I want.* His threats and demands drained me emotionally and physically. I spent five months in my nursing course before deciding to quit. I simply couldn't keep up with everything, and the pressure at home was unbearable.

Thankfully, my friend Laura worked at a convent caring for the sick, and she helped me secure a position there. Within a week, I started working night shifts. Though exhausting, I was relieved to have a steady job. However, working nights and being unable to sleep properly during the day soon took its toll.

Tony's disregard for his responsibilities, especially towards the children, became glaringly apparent. One day, Max, who was five years old, and baby Natatsha, then just eight months old, were home with him while I ran an errand. When I returned, I found Max at the top of the stairs, holding the baby carriage with Natatsha inside, ready to push it down. My heart stopped. I yelled and rushed to grab the carriage.

—*Where's your father?* I asked in panic.

Max answered innocently, —*He's sleeping.*

Sure enough, Tony was asleep in his room, oblivious to the danger his children were in. I was furious but powerless to make him understand the gravity of his neglect.

Between my night shifts and the endless household responsibilities, I was running on fumes. Tony worked during the day, Jacques in the evening, and I at night. In the mornings, when I came home, Jacques would be there, letting me catch a little sleep. I'd wake up around noon, and sometimes we'd share moments of intimacy before he left for work at 3 o'clock. I'd then prepare dinner so that Tony could eat when he returned at 5 p.m.

After dinner, Tony would go out, only to return around 10 p.m., often demanding intimacy right before I left for my night shift. It was unbearable. I felt trapped, physically and emotionally. Every night, after finishing my work, I would kneel and pray, pleading with God for a way out. Tony's threats to harm me if I left loomed over me, but deep inside, I knew my escape was only a matter of time.

Soon, Tony's daughter Célia arrived. We picked her up from the airport, and I was genuinely happy to meet her. She was quiet and shy, but we got along well. I explained the household routines to her, helped her adjust to life in this new country, and ensured she was registered for school.

Because the school year had already begun, she was placed in a special class. Despite the challenges, Célia adapted quickly and never caused any trouble. She even helped me with chores around the house, which lightened my load somewhat.

Tony, unsurprisingly, paid little attention to his daughter, leaving her care entirely to me. This added complexity to my already strained situation. Jacques and I had to be discreet, waiting for moments when Célia wasn't home to share even the simplest expressions of affection.

The Separation

The Christmas holidays of 1974 were a turning point in my life. Tony and Jacques were on vacation, but I was working through the holidays, with a planned break for New Year's. On Christmas morning, after a brief rest at home, I went with Tony, Jacques, and Célia to visit my children, Max and Natatsha, at Madame Bélisle's. We brought them gifts, and their happiness lifted my spirits despite my exhaustion. Since I was overwhelmed, I asked Madame Bélisle to keep Natatsha for a little longer but brought Max home to spend the rest of the holidays with us.

Back home, the atmosphere remained tense. Tony was distant and inattentive, leaving much of the burden on me. Célia, on the other hand, was adjusting well and had started school across the street. However, the looming arrival of Tony's sister—who disliked me and was an enemy of Jacques—made me realize that drastic changes were necessary. Jacques warned me, —*If you don't leave, I'm leaving.* It was clear: I had to act.

One Saturday evening, while at work, I felt my exhaustion reach its peak. My head throbbed, and a voice inside me urged, —*It's time to act.* I made a plan to confess everything to Tony, hoping it would be my way out. Before I finished my shift, I tried calling Jacques to explain my intentions, but there was no answer. With no other choice, I called Tony to pick me up—a rare occurrence, as I almost never asked him for rides.

When Tony arrived, I greeted him with an unusual warmth. Once in the car, I told him not to start the engine.

—*I have something to tell you,* I said.

He looked confused but listened.

—*Tony, Natatsha is not your daughter. She's Jacques' daughter. Jacques and I have been in love for a long time. I've never loved you, and I can't do this anymore. I want to leave your house. You can keep everything.*

The words tumbled out, and with them, a weight lifted from my chest. For the first time, I felt free from the secret that had consumed me for years.

Tony sat motionless, his mouth slightly open, unable to respond. When he finally spoke, his words surprised me.

—*You can't leave. This is your home. Let's go back and talk about this.*

When we returned home, I went straight to Jacques' room. He was asleep and woke up startled as I told him what had happened. —*This isn't how it was supposed to happen!* he exclaimed, burying his head in his hands. I assured him that it was better this way and asked him to admit the truth if Tony questioned him.

Tony wasted no time. He called Jacques to the dining room and demanded confirmation. Jacques simply said, —*Yes, it's true,*‖ before adding, —*I'll leave this house this afternoon.*‖ He then retreated to his room to pack.

Tony tried to persuade me to stay, saying, —*I'll forget everything, but you can't see Jacques anymore. Stay here; this is your home.*‖ His calm demeanor was unsettling. Deep down, I suspected he had known about my relationship with Jacques all along but chose to ignore it because Jacques was contributing financially.

That evening, after Jacques left, Tony's true nature resurfaced. He assaulted me, asserting, —*I'll bed you as long as I want, and you'll never leave me.*‖ I cried through the night, resolved to escape.

Tony's sister was scheduled to arrive in two days. Her arrival was the final push I needed to leave. The next morning, after dropping Tony at work, I called Jacques and explained my plan. Then, I reached out to Sister Berthe and my sister Irène for support. Both encouraged me to leave immediately, and my sister offered me refuge at her place.

I told Max about our departure. Despite being sick with the flu, he was eager to help and excited to see Jacques again. Together, we packed only our essentials—clothes, curtains, and dishes gifted by my sister—and left everything else behind. Jacques and I loaded our cars and moved my belongings to my sister's and cousin's homes.

Before leaving, I parked Tony's car outside his workplace, leaving the keys and a note:

—*Since your sister is arriving, and you absolutely want her to live with us, I have decided to leave. I've taken our son and gone to my sister's. We will not return. I left the furniture and everything else, including the bank account.*

That evening, Tony called, furious. He threatened me, saying, —*If you don't come back, everyone will abandon you.* But I was resolute. I warned him to contact me only through my lawyer, which enraged him further.

I then called Madame Bélisle to inform her of my decision and asked her to care for Max and Natatsha. Despite my exhaustion, I worked that night, but my fatigue was overwhelming. The head nurse, noticing my condition, granted me a few days off and offered me a day shift position, which I gladly accepted.

The next morning, I brought Max to Madame Bélisle's house. She welcomed me with warmth and kindness, offering me food and a place to rest. For the first time in weeks, I allowed myself to cry. I poured out my story to her, and she listened with compassion, her presence a balm to my weary soul.

That night, I slept deeply, feeling the weight of the past few days begin to lift. When I awoke, I was greeted with coffee and her gentle smile. Her support and care rejuvenated me, giving me the strength to face the challenges ahead.

Epilogue

A Conclusion of Sorts

The wall has been crossed. For many years, through these twelve lives—filled with moments of happiness and instances of extreme violence against my identity—I lacked both the opportunity and courage to truly examine how I was living or to reflect on the events unfolding around me. This inability kept me from fully understanding my own culture and the cultures of the countries I passed through. By revisiting the past, I sought first to understand myself, and then to make sense of others. It was a challenging journey, but one that has allowed me to look ahead with greater clarity.

Writing this book was vital to me. It helped me regain my bearings and share my feelings with others. I have always dreamed of writing. I love reading and writing; they fuel my imagination. When I write, I feel a deep sense of peace, as if nothing else exists. Everything unfolds within me. At times, I act in ways that others don't understand, and I've come to realize there is another part of me—a second self— that I am constantly seeking to understand. It is this search for inner clarity that enables me to live more fully.

My life has been marked by hardships, from my childhood to my adolescence and into adulthood. I've learned that life is far from an easy road. I've encountered cruelty, but I've also seen how joy can unexpectedly arise amidst sorrow. Despite my naivete, I have come to understand that happiness is real. It can be created, and hope, while elusive, is not always an illusion.

I now understand those who choose not to revisit their past, preferring to forget, as I once tried to do. But in retracing my steps, I've realized that avoidance is its own form of captivity. Behind me are twelve distinct periods—twelve lives—each like a chapter marking a break in my existence. Revisiting them was a way to seek answers to questions that haunted me. I've witnessed the abrupt collapse of happiness and the coexistence of good and evil.

Each of us possesses an inner voice—a clear and simple guide that too often we suppress. This voice, honest and unwavering, demands our attention. It offers the means to achieve balance and freedom, to discover the essence of who we are. Yet, we fear ourselves and resist its clarity.

On this Earth, it is up to us to create our happiness. No one else will build it for us. True happiness, when we allow it, can support us like a comforting hand extended in kinship. I believe this deeply because it has strengthened and shaped me. Happiness is not just in the fleeting moments of joy but in the good times we carry in our memory. These moments endure, even when life seems to unravel. They remain within us, waiting to be relived when we need them most. And so, life continues.

Generic

The cast of my life Parents

Estelle and Frantz

Children

Max (Bitou) Natatsha

Sisters and brothers

Irène Robert Julien

Half-sister and half-brothers

(father's side)

Claire Alain Raymond

Claude Marcel

Nephew

Rivard

Alain's wife

Ida

Aunts

Anna, my mother's sister

Dadia, my father's sister

Dieula, my mother's adoptive sister Annie

Dadia's mother

Madame Médé

Uncle (mother's side)

Joseph

Friends of my mother

Mrs.Légère Ruth, my godmother

Yongo, neighbour

Friend of my sister

Christiane

Cousins

Viviane

Suzie

Fabienne

Sola

Gisèle

Julia

My father's mistress

Vanité

Teacher (grade school)

Martha

Generic

Childhood friends

Sylvain

Doris

Violette

Yanik

Nélia

Josie

Lovers

Sylvain

Henry

Tony

Jacques

The mystery lover

Nuns (in Haiti)

Sister Berthe

Sister Marie Marthe

Sister Jeanne

Nun's employees

Jeannette

Marie

Laura

Amédé

Boarders

Collette

Joséphine

Miche

Maguy

Josie

Witnesses for the 1st marriage

Dadia

Georges

Servants (Haiti)

Thérésa

Zita

Lisette

Stay in New York

Aunts

Dadia

Annie

Anna

Brother

Alain

Friends

Érik

Isabelle

Louky

Metty

The good Samaritan

An American

MONTREAL

Enice's relatives

Irène (sister)

Robert (brother)

Gisèle (cousin)

Viviane (cousin)

Generic

Viviane's daughter

Micha

Tony's relatives

Célia (daughter)

Édith (sister)

Rosita (cousin)

Friends

Nélia

Danie

Dona

Viviane

Laura

Robert

Mrs Maurice

Jean

Simon

Maddy

Clauré

Viala

Sitters (nannies)

Mrs. Fara

Mrs. Léon

Mrs. Liliane Bélisle

Liliane's daughter

Francine

Viala's baby

Yvi

Where are we at?

Times change, and somehow nothing changes.

One who refuses change is often judged badly and left on the way side.

We say that no light can be perceived without darkness, yet certain animals see very clearly through the darkest nights.

The lost dog will always manage to find its way. It is a completely different story, that of the man

who is blinded by change and not by the light.

Perhaps we do have something fundamental to learn from these innocent animals, for times change, but nothing changes.

Max (Bitou)

Nature is human

Like the tulip's liveliness,

Being a girl who has become a woman, a motherand finally mature,Life chooses you,

For your purity, for your naivety.

The tulip dies during the cold seasons And is reborn during the warm seasons.Life chooses you,

To come through its highs and lows.

Today, life is once more offering you its highs.The tulip is always reborn, in the image of the moment when she was a girl.Life chooses you.

Natatsha

Acknowledgements

Not often have I had the opportunity to thank the people who have helped us. I am taking advantage of this book's publishing to do so.

First of all I want to thank with all of my heart my sister Irène. When we were children, after the death of our mother, she was always there to take care of us during the difficult times, despite her young age. I also want to thank my brother Robert.

I also want to offer my thanks to aunt Dadia, amongst others for having helped me during my first marriage. Also thanks to the nuns who gave us a helping hand for the reception.

As for aunt Dieula, I will never forget what she has done for us. No other member of the family has matched her generosity and her devotion on our behalf.

I will also never be able to forget Liliane Bélisle. I love her a lot and I am expressing to her my gratitude for everything she has done for my children and me. She has been more than a mother.

I also thank my two children, Max and Natatsha, for having helped me to make this dream come true and for having supported me during the whole process of writing this book. A special gratitude testimonial to Natatsha who, on top of having to take care of her two children and her business, has always found the time and the way to encour-age me to go on.

It is important for me to also express my most sincere thanks to Sister Berthe who, at my side or from afar, has constantly accompanied me.

Finally, I am expressing my gratitude to the people who took the time to read my text at different stages of the editing process: Tom Levitt, Maude Martineau, Lucette Martineau, Hélène Gallant, Line Gareau, Anna Gerda, Seema Arora and Sister Rachel.

Thank you to Caroline Léger for her advice and her help during the editing. Finally, I give special thanks to Koralie Woodward as well as to Jean-Simon Brisebois.

Enice Toussaint

Readers' Comments

During the preparation of A Woman Amongst Others, many people were invited to read the book or its summary. Here we are transcribing a few of the commentaries, which were forwarded to us afterwards.

I have journeyed with Enice and I have accompanied her through joy, difficulty, struggles, searches. Her ardour and consistency in attempting to free herself from her bewitchments and the means taken to discover the paths of light have brought her to a greater maturity; she is now a more joyful woman, dedicated and always ready to pray; she is a mother happy to have a son and a daughter who travel by her side. Her immense joy is to be a grandmother of three adorable grandchildren.

Sister Berthe

—In my numerous books, the Haitian woman (a young sensual girl, mother or grand-mother) plays an important role, but I am pleased to hear her voice for once.

Excerpt from commentary written by Dany Laferriere, a Quebec novelist of Haitian origin.

Dany Laferrière

I traveled the pages with sustained eagerness and intense curiosity.

In the beginning, I thought the author's life was in peril, that she would never complete her testimony. But as I got into the heart of the subject, I understood that this woman has suffered because she is too sensitive.

Furthermore, Enice Toussaint is a great lover of peo- ple and of life. I consider that this autobiography is to be recommended to all women, of all classes of society.

Anne, reader and friend

My dear Enice, what I am feeling, is the need to talk, to tell your story to people who burely know you and to those with whom you live on a daily basis, and to those who do not even know you.

The manner in which you described your childhood is wonderful. There does not seem to be much that you have left out. We get the impression that you are transmitting a message without telling others what to do.

Without a doubt the people who will have the privilege of reading your autobiography will be able to step back into their past while questioning themselves. There is no age limit to question ourselves, everyone has the possibility to do so.

Gerda C.

I believe that the author gives us very well the over-whelming aspect of the situation that she is living which might seem difficult to understand. In fact, I get lost in my personal impressions of the narrative...

The end is a great big breath of fresh air, it is a phys-ical experience. This is why I find that the theme of liberty is central in this narrative; the narrator has undertaken a long quest to reach it.

As the author says herself, the end makes you feel good in thanks for having distanced herself from the past. She has been solely responsible for her liberation.

Maude Martineau

What I thought was most interesting was the author's belief in God and how she viewed Him as her confidant. Her strong faith is inspirational. Also I felt a lot of sympathy when she described the numerous difficulties she has experienced.... it's a very good book.

Anne, reader and friend

A testimony of moving sincerity and of rare authentic-ity. What first struck me in Enice's narrative, is the candour manifested by the storyteller from the very first lines of the text. The result: we keep a constant interest for the story, told in an alert and unflourished style. Up until the last page we are overcome by the most contradictory feelings: irrita- tion and compassion, revolt and tenderness, resentment andsolidarity.

A Woman Amongst Others is above all else an extre- mely courageous undertaking, which dares to bare for all to see the failings and insufficiencies of the Haitian woman and of the Haitian men. It will offend well-meaning souls, but its reading reveals itself indispensable for all the people who will not be blinded by their prejudice and who desire the progress of the human species.

Lionel Jean

I have read the summary of Enice's book. I am deeply touched by her story and very impressed with the narra- tive's simplicity. It is well written and we find in it many emotions. I am looking forward to reading her book.

I believe that this book will have a positive impact on most women

Tale of a multifaceted life by Enice Toussaint

is the first of three volumes published by Éditions Nouveau Siècle.

For information or to contact Natatsha Casimir.

Please visit: www.enspublishing.com

Email: Ediontionsens@gmail.com

like my mother and it will most probably sen- sitise men a little more towards women. I can imagine the courage and the faith that was required of Enice to write this book. I want to congratulate her for this source of inspi-ration that she shares with us and for the many testimoniesthat are found in her book.

Gerson

www.ingramcontent.com/pod-product-compliance
Lightning Source LLC
Chambersburg PA
CBHW041304240426
43661CB00011B/1019